THIS BOOK
BELONGS TO

....

....

Thank you for Purchasing my book and taking the time to read it from front to back. I am always grateful when a reader chooses my work and I hope you enjoyed it!

With the vast selection available online, I am touched that you chose to be purchasing my work and take valuable time out of your life to read it. My hope is that you feel you made the right decision.

I very much would like to know what you thought of the book. Please take the time to write an honest and informative review on Amazon.com. Your experience and opinions will be of great benefit to me and those readers looking to make an informed choice.

With much thanks.

@COPYRIGHT 2024

The content contained within this book may not be reproduced, duplicated, or transmitted without direct written permission from the author or the publisher. Under no circumstances will any blame or legal responsibility be held against the publisher, or author, for any damages, reparation, or monetary loss due to the information contained within this book. Either directly or indirectly.

Legal Notice:

This book is copyright protected. This book is only for personal use. You cannot amend, distribute, sell, use, quote, or paraphrase any part, or the content within this book, without the consent of the author or publisher.

Disclaimer Notice:

Please note the information contained within this document is for educational and entertainment purposes only. All effort has been executed to present accurate, up-to-date, and reliable, complete information. No warranties of any kind are declared or implied. Readers acknowledge that the author is not engaging in the rendering of legal, financial, medical, or professional advice. The content within this book has been derived from various sources. Please consult a licensed professional before attempting any techniques outlined in this book. By reading this document, the reader agrees that under no circumstances is the author responsible for any losses, direct or indirect, which are incurred as a result of the use of the information contained within this document, including, but not limited to — errors, omissions, or inaccuracies.

Table of Contents

Introduction	5
Chapter One: Initial Idea	8
Chapter Two: Business Plan	17
Chapter Three: Finances Sorted	31
Chapter Four: Finding A Mentor - Learn from the Experience of Others & Know Your Limits	42
Chapter Five: The Company You Keep - Who Is Going on The Journey with You?	50
Chapter Six: The Legal Status of Your Business Now and In the Future	59
Chapter Seven: Your Business Is Born; Naming, Registering, And Insuring Your Business	68
Chapter Eight: Hiring Team Members	78
Chapter Nine: Marketing & Promoting	87
Chapter Ten: Scaling & Growing	96
Conclusion	105

Introduction

Nearly all modern startups are made on a whim.

Entrepreneurship is now becoming a recurrent phenomenon among youth looking to reinvent the future. It's not uncommon to hear of ambitious youth completely heedless of boundaries and filled with remarkable enthusiasm, deciding to start a business in the comfort of their dorm and in the trust-worthy company of future co-founders.

Oftentimes, an idea comes to mind when entrepreneurs run into a problem they cannot immediately overcome. That's when they come up with a solution themselves, and the solution becomes a million-dollar idea for a business. The idea eventually booms into a business and experiences early success. It's rise to glory is plastered all over the news and inspires millions of people.

And that's where the problem comes in.

The simplistic and overly-generic explanation of an entrepreneur's success leaves many optimists thinking that all starting a business takes is an idea. But the business world has never been completely reliant on just creativity – in fact, many successful businesses lack in that area, but do just fine.

Possibly the most common underlying cause of startup failure is lack of a good strategy (which is usually comprised of far more tedious details than innovative ideas). That's not to say that innovation is irrelevant to the success of a business, but no fledgling business can operate without a realistic plan that assesses the number of potential customers it can bring during its infant stages – enough to get the company to stand on its own feet.

Young entrepreneurs are exposed to a plethora of success stories in magazines and blockbuster movies that emphasize the importance of perseverance and a flair for rebellion against the current norm. Those traits may contribute to success, but the stories often leave out the mundane procedures that ground businesses and make them last more than a few years.

You don't come across a news piece about the accountant that did more than prepare reports good enough to survive a surprise audit. Nor do you hear of what type of contract was signed to prevent a founder from being stuck with a partner who nearly destroyed company finances with poor management. That said, it's unlikely management is brought up at all. This reduces the complex equation of business politics and arrangements into this abstract notion of hard work and perseverance.

But that isn't to say that starting a business is all that challenging; it's probably easier than you think, if you know what you're doing and take the time to familiarize yourself with the dull intricacies alongside the more pleasant stages of innovation.

The trick is to know exactly what you're in for before you step into the game. You don't start by introducing your idea to an investor before taking the time to learn about the processes for which you and your potential partners must prepare. Model implementation and product definition must of necessity lead to the less-fun stages of paperwork and financing.

While starting a business has risks, it's never a gamble; it's a process that can be taught, and that's what this book aims to do. Don't think of yourself as an entrepreneur who's about to test their luck with a game of fortune. It's quite likely that your product or service has a demographic somewhere, and all it takes is for you to get a grasp on how to reach your target market efficiently.

With that said, it's best to get some facts and myths out of the way before we delve further into this book; let's strip down the Hollywood/tabloid images of entrepreneurship that may fog your journey to success.

Startups do not mean product-making in a dimly-lit garage. No matter where you decide to develop your idea, you need to understand than starting your company takes more than just a definition of your product. With a new and innovative product comes an equally innovative method to manage it. You are not just building a product, but an institution that can sell your product to the right people.

It's also not a matter of finalizing your idea and introducing it to the public. To up your chances of success, your product needs to be experimented on and introduced to a small group of users that will give you honest feedback. The process of starting a business isn't just a method of making a living and revolutionizing the industry; it's also a process of learning from your users how to render your idea into a product that will be appealing to your customers.

This doesn't mean you have to tailor your product to the opinions of the test- group – at least, not in the exact manner they ask. You could be told that your service or product is faulty due to a particular aspect, but sometimes those who test your product will perceive a unique aspect as a flaw when it's only misunderstood and needs to be better explained.

Lastly, you need to understand that innovation doesn't just boil down to business models and product features. You're going to have to innovate in other areas, like financing, being able to measure your progress, and gauging the potential scale of your success.

And because we want to help you build a solid plan that you can confidently follow, our guide will help you recognize indicators of early success and make sure you don't get caught up in the excitement of developing an idea to the point that you forget to get a handle on rendering it a useful tool to the public.

Techniques and advice in this book are based on real methods that successful startups have used. They will allow you to skip the methodologies which are more likely to fail, and get straight to those that are nearly guaranteed to get you through the phase of "starting up" and into that of implementing and launching.

Chapter One: Initial Idea

Starting and running a business requires courage, drive, and, of course, a lot of planning. If you are reading this, you surely possess the former two because this is a serious business (pun intended). The thought of starting a company has crossed almost everyone's mind, but only a handful put in the time, effort, and hard work required in the planning stage.

This chapter will cover all the aspects of coming up with your business idea (or the practicality of one you already have). It will give you insights and assurance about your concept before you go ahead with it. After all, your idea is the foundation and character of your business.

Asking questions about yourself and your convictions, being convinced about your idea, planning it, and analyzing it practically are the first few steps you can take to frame this essential primary stage.

Question and Evaluate Yourself

If you are determined enough to begin, you need first to question yourself as to why you want to start a business. The answer needs to be more than escaping a routine nine-to-five job, and it should be honest because you need to work with it for the rest of your life. Questioning yourself will diminish the failure probability of your business because you will know whether you can stick to it long-term and put in all the exhausting work to get it to the top.

Questions like…

- Why exactly do you want to open a business when you know the efforts, capital, and time it will require? Is it because you want to be your own boss, or solely because of the financial rewards you would get?

- Do you have enough capital to manage the initial costs?

- If you are working a stable job, are you willing to take the risk of quitting, and put all your time and effort into establishing your business?
- Do you already have an idea for your business? Why would you like to follow that particular concept?
- Are you able to handle pressure in a stressful environment?
- Will you be okay without a helping hand? Can you find solutions to problems on your own? Can you make quick decisions?
- Are you proficient enough to manage a team and give instructions?
- What outcomes do you expect from your business?
- Where do you see yourself and your company in the next five years?
- Are you willing to follow your formulated plan to reach that point?
- Is your objective solely to earn money, or do you also want to develop and learn along the way?
- Have you considered the circumstances in case you fail? Will you be formulating a back-up plan for that possibility?

If you are completely honest with yourself, this checklist will help you determine whether running a business would be a disaster or a piece of cake for you. You can also make a pros-and-cons list to detect your strengths and weaknesses. If you feel that your weaknesses won't drastically affect your work, you can work on them along the way. For example, if you are unable to give proper instructions to your team, you can hire a team head or manager who can direct them, helping you learn this skill while working with them.

Evaluating yourself will give you a translucent glimpse of how well you will manage your business. If you are finding excuses for not starting your own business, it simply means that you aren't confident enough to begin. Perhaps you think the economy is in too bad a shape to start a business? There's never a "bad season" to start a business. In fact, running a company during economic downturns can eliminate competition, thus increasing the demand for your services. You can capture more clients when they have fewer options from which to choose. Also, depending on your type of business, you can have the added benefit of purchasing tools and equipment at lower prices. See, there's always a brighter side to any issue.

This exercise of listing your fears or problems and finding solutions to each can help you gain more confidence and prepare you for the worst. You need to talk to people who are already established within your discipline and are willing to help. Conduct a thorough market analysis as well; we'll talk about that in detail later.

Contemplate Your Business Idea and Concept

To begin, you need an idea, a solid concept. More importantly, you need to reason out why you would like to get into that particular niche.

If you already have an idea in mind and are determined to follow it, there's no point in waiting; it only makes sense to follow through and move on to the next steps.

But if you don't have a concept yet, there's no need to worry. Here are a few ways to help you to generate your big business idea;

these tips will also help you elevate your idea if you are already fixed on one.

Dig into Your Skills and Interests

Your personal interests, hobbies, or skills can turn into great business ideas; not only will you get your business running much more passionately, but you will also thoroughly enjoy your work. Make a list of all your interests in one column and your skills in the other. They do not have to be remarkable; it's alright to possess a weird interest or skill if it's one that keeps you captivated. Rank them according to your preference, keeping the business aspect in mind. Match up any interests and skills that go hand-in-hand or complement each other. Skill-and-interest combinations can make for exceptional business concepts. For instance, your interest in food and your baking skills combined could lead you to run a patisserie or a café. If you are skilled in art and adore stationery, you could start a stationery subscription box that reaches out to potential artists every month.

A business concept generated out of your interests and hobbies creates the drive to work hard and put in more effort; moreover, you will earn money from it. As they say, "Turn your hobby into a profession, and you will never have to work." Doing something that grasps your interest creates the benefit of extra care put into the work.; you will never lack motivation, push yourself more to make a difference, and be identified as a passionate entrepreneur that is changing the world one step at a time.

Think About Problems You Face Everyday

Issues in your personal life, business, and personality can also be a source of ideas. For instance, there might be things that you dislike or are unmanageable in your daily life such as the inconvenience of traveling to work, not being able to manage daily cooking and weekly grocery-shopping, struggling with crappy internet, or seeing a flat tire on your car. Solutions: an affordable cab service, a grocery/food delivery app that gets you healthy inexpensive meals, a reliable internet connection service, and a car repair service that can send a nearby mechanic to change the tire. There you have four potential ideas from four everyday problems.

'Think more positively' is a motto to abide by at this stage. Rest assured that you are not the only one dealing with such issues; millions of other working-class people are seeking solutions to such annoyances and are willing to pay in return for additional help that can make their lives easier. Talk to people; list the problems they face in their personal and business lives, compare notes, and you will find potential business ideas right under your nose.

If you are aiming towards solving a problem rather than just earning money, your audience will grow rapidly; if you are selling a product that is needed rather than wanted, you already have their attention. Presenting a solution to a problem that needs immediate attention will turn your business into something that matters to the general public.

Look for Disciplines That Are in Demand

It is also feasible to choose an idea based on recent demands in certain product or service markets, which can make your business an overnight success. If you are not among those who want to find a niche based on their skills, you need to research the latest appeals. For example, fashion is not your forte, but opening an online fashion store with all the best brands can gain traction quickly in the teens-to-young-adults market.

This is another reason why people fear beginning a business; they feel it means inventing something or being the pioneer in their arena. Yes, standing out does matter, but it's not worth dumping a good plan due to the absence of a newly created gimmick. You can smartly pick your niche by searching for high-demand and low-supply fields.

Ask yourself, "How can I make it better?" or "Is there a potential sub-category that can be added to this venue?" Make sure you have done thorough homework about the idea because there might be sensible reasons why there are only a few established companies in a high-demand market. Perhaps the problems are solvable but require a lot of effort which few are willing to make.

If you need to learn a new skill, enroll yourself in a course; if you need to gather huge capital, borrow or take a loan. Just make it happen. You will be extremely grateful and satisfied in the long run to have put in all the effort to push your company to success.

If the constraints seem almost impossible to overcome, solicit professional help. If you have tried your best but cannot make it happen, you might have to rethink that particular idea.

Find Inspiration

There are significant factors within your surroundings that go unnoticed by most. You need to pay attention and constantly observe to find an inspiration that will completely change the game. It could hit you anywhere, in the oddest ways; in a park, in your kitchen, scrolling through social media, or even on the toilet. Seeing the people jogging in the park, concerned about their health and fitness might inspire you to open a fitness center or hire a yoga instructor for your gym; looking at piled-up garbage might lead to you an idea for reducing waste by opening a package-free service which will reduce waste and plastic.

This unconventional method of searching for an idea is not only useful for the beginners but also for those who are fixed on an idea or are already running a stable business. Adding more products or subcategories to your venue can promote your business and help it gain a new identity. Also, tweaking your existing services and reframing them can bring you more clients. Keep an eye out for what people want and what they would like.

Travel can produce business ideas. It's not feasible to travel all the time to find inspiration and ideas; we are just suggesting you take advantage of any opportunity to travel when you get it. You will get to learn about new people, cultures, and ways of living. Suppose you take a trip to Japan and get completely fascinated with the food and culture. You could come back home and research potential business ideas in the area of Japanese food and culture. You could end up opening a ramen and matcha food truck, import Japanese goods and sell them online, or get inspired by traditional Japanese clothing and design a sub-category in your already-established fashion store. The possibilities are endless.

Reading books is another way to travel; it increases knowledge and directs you onto new paths. Flipping through magazines or browsing the internet can lead to brain-storming sessions that lead to an idea. Think, contemplate, come up with an idea or improvement, and stick to it.

Market Research

Once you are content with your idea and excited to start following it, you need to analyze it by conducting market analysis, research, and surveys, or by seeking advice from fellow business-owners. This step will ensure the viability of your idea.

Say, for instance, your idea is to open a cleaning service. You can run a market analysis on the existing number of cleaning businesses in your area, the percentage of successful or renowned establishments, and their years in business. List and compare their service types, their hourly or per-square-foot rate patterns, hours of operation, types of clientele, and other criteria. This will help you chart out the success rate of that type of business in your area and indicate your chances of a favorable outcome.

This applies to any idea; research the competition within your niche. Doing this will also help you to frame a business model for your services, such as lashing down rates, providing promotional codes and coupons, developing an application, or coming up with additional perks that can attract customers. It will not only bring you more customers initially but also authorize your name in the market. The idea is to stand out; people need to be confident in hiring you over others because you are different and better.

Again, answering a relevant set of questions for this step can also help you predict how well your business idea will run.

- Are you offering different services than others in your vicinity?
  - If not, what is the level of competition, and how does your idea stand out?
  - Are there feasible ways to make your service better?
  - Who will be your target audience?
  - How will you make your company more accessible to your customers?
  - Will your clientele willingly pay for your services?
  - Will your investment receive substantial returns within an ideal time period?

As we said, it's okay not to have a completely distinctive idea if your approach is to make amendments and changes that will make your product or service stand out. A proper business plan can serve to merely adorn your idea, which we'll talk more about it later.

Another important aspect to consider is your target audience, and how easily they can access your services. You need to analyze whether your clientele is more open to technology and website usage or to speaking on a phone. If you are targeting the younger audience, say between 20 to 35 years, your services would be more accessible through a website. If your audience is older, phone calls or scheduling meetings is better for them. Surveys and statistics based on the reachability of your service can help you develop your idea accordingly.

Fixing your rates in a smart manner is also essential in the starting stage because your products or services are not tested by any of your clients yet, and so there is no proof of how genuine and good they are. You might want to strategize your prices according to the current market value to gain more clients in the beginning. If you provide top-notch services, they are bound to come back and spread the word.

Next, work out an analysis of the capital you will invest in your idea and the probable return on the investment. Take the help of financial advisors to determine the income and cash flow, and the anticipated time period of the initial cost. We will talk more about the finances, running rates, and capital part of your business in the following chapters of this book.

Most importantly, build an excellent network that can educate you about things of which you may have been completely unaware. Since you are new to running a business, guidance and insights from experts can be invaluable in helping you learn better ways to handle problems and meet the needs of your customers. You will learn the secret behind the mantra, "Work smarter, not harder."

No business idea is too big or too small. If you have what it takes and are ready to put in what is required, you can turn a small and insignificant idea into a revenue-generating machine. Above all, question yourself; be honest, trust your instincts, gather courage, be practical and confident, believe in yourself, and unravel your potential. You've got this.

In the coming chapters, you will learn how to push your business idea forward by forming a business plan, engaging the legal procedures, and developing ways to promote your business once it is up-and-running.

Chapter Two: Business Plan

There's a quote known throughout the world of business:

"If you fail to plan, you plan to fail."

Your business plan can be the single most important factor that determines how successful your business is going to be. If you think this an exaggeration, wait until the end of this chapter and think again.

So, if it's such an important thing, what exactly is a business plan? Let's get right into it.

What Is a Business Plan and Why Is It Important?

Your business plan covers every aspect of your business; it includes everything from why you're thinking about creating this business to the opportunity you found in the market to the market analysis, marketing strategy, financial plan, your business structure, and everything in between and beyond.

Creating a business plan is the most critical thing you need to do right away, for three good reasons.

The first reason is that your business plan is going to act as your road map. It will be the guide that you'll religiously follow in every step of your business, from research and development to launching your business and hiring your team. The more effort and detail you put into it, the clearer and more reliable your plan will be.

The second reason is that if you have no idea what to write in your plan just yet, then this is when you *most* need to devise your business plan. You don't have to know everything; once you start on your plan, you'll find that there are way too many aspects of the business you're trying to create that you had no idea you should even consider. You'll be forced to start looking beyond what you know. Not only will you gain invaluable insights into how to properly launch your business but you'll also question your initial idea, examine different practices in the market, and start on more solid ground.

Finally, the third reason is that once you start the operations of your business, you'll inevitably lose focus on (or entirely forget) many of the finer details - unless you have everything on paper. And having your thoughts on paper is completely different from having a perfectly written and well-articulated plan at your disposal. This plan will not only act as your guide and a reminder of important details but ll also serve as the proof of your conscientious preparation to present to investors, potential partners, and others in other kinds of business relations.

Before Starting Your Business Plan

Before getting started on your plan, there a few things that you should do first.

Widen Your Scope with Research

Research is going to be your best companion on the journey of devising your plan. You're going to research your business idea, the businesses you'll be competing with, your marketing strategy, your target audience - and you'll have to look through a lot of statistics, best practices, and advice. Whatever you know, your research will fortify it or present you with better alternatives. Whatever you don't know, you'll get to know through research. We can't stress how important research is!

Decide Why You're Writing this Plan

There are many reasons to write a business plan, and you need to define yours. Are you seeking investment? If so, what kind of investors are you targeting, and in what aspects will they be most interested? You'll want to give them everything they need, without beating around the bush too much. Are you creating this plan for your team members, so that they can have a clearer idea of their role? Do you need this business plan for your own sake, as your road map and reference manual? The reason you're writing the business will guide your research and the road you take in creating the plan.

Be Detailed, but Avoid Exaggerating Your Plan

The more detailed the plan, the better. However, there's a difference between attention to details and redundant over-use of information. Your business plan should include all the important aspects of your business, in much detail; after all, it *is* your road map. But once you start cramming in information for the sake of increasing the number of your pages, you're just wasting time. Remember, you don't have to write a 100-page plan. A solid, bulletproof, backed-up plan of 10 pages can prove to be much more useful than a 100-page plan that gets you lost every time you look at it.

Research Business Plans and Choose One

When it comes to creating a business plan, there are different schools of thought. Many startups choose to go with a lean start-up plan, using the Business Model Canvas (BMC) or its even leaner "modified version". Others go for traditional business templates that are more detailed. You can choose either form to get started, but sooner or later, you'll figure out that both methods complement each other. We recommend that you start with a BMC and then devise your detailed business plan.

Creating Your Business Model Canvas

A BMC contains nine key elements:

Key Partnerships

In this section, you list all the partners that will be essential for the operations of your business; your strategic partners, which include manufacturers, suppliers, contractors, and others. You'll also list why they'd be interested in partnering up with you.

Key Activities

What kind of activities does your business rely on in its operation? These are the activities that reflect your value proposition, your vision, and your goals. They're also the activities that will benefit your business in its competitive advantage over others.

Value Proposition

Why is your business important? Why should it be out in the market? What need does it fill, or what opportunity does it serve? Your value proposition is the core value your business provides to its customers.

Customer Relationship

How will you be contacting your customers? How will they contact you? Will your business be automated online, will you deal with them physically, or is a mix of both? Is that how your target segment expects your customer relationship to be, or do they prefer other alternatives?

Customer Segment

Whom will you be targeting with your products and services? Are they men, women, or both? Are you targeting adults, kids, or parents? Which class are you targeting? If you're targeting more than one segment, then which is your most important customer?

Key Resources

These are the resources you'll need to use to create value for your customers. Your key resources can include capital, team members, equipment, or even intellectual property.

Distribution Channels

How will you reach your customers? Do you have a physical product that needs to be shipped? Do you have a customer-service department that keeps in contact with your customers? If so, then how does the communication work? Which are the most effective channels, how much do they cost, and how do they fit into your operational plan?

Cost Structure

This section includes details about the ongoing costs of running your business, including daily operational costs, payroll, periodical subscriptions, and any other recurrent costs. Next, you'll pinpoint the most expensive resources and/or activities; from there you can decide whether you want to focus on cutting down costs or improving value.

Revenue Stream

Arguably the most important aspect of any business is: how will you make money? What values do you provide that your customers will be willing to pay for? How will they pay? There can be more than more one revenue stream and different strategies for profit, all of which you should list here.

Your Business Plan: A Step-By-Step Guide

Moving on to your business plan, here are the most essential elements in any business plan:

Executive Summary

Your executive summary is the most important part of your plan. It should be the first thing that any potential lenders or investors see, but it's the part that you're going to write after you finish up all the other parts of your plan.

Your executive summary should convey your passion, goals, vision, and the most important aspects of your plan. Anyone reading it should feel excited about reading the rest of the plan; if they're not, there's a problem.

Typically, your executive summary will include the following:

- A brief introduction to your business; essentially a description of your company (its Vision and Mission Statement), its key products and/or services, and your goals in creating this business

- Your target market(s)

-

- Your competitive advantage
- An overview of your team and its qualifications
- A financial outlook that describes the capital you need, how you'll utilize it, and how you'll turn it into profits.

Company Description

Your company description includes the following points:

Mission Statement

What's the main value and purpose of your business? It shouldn't take more than one or two sentences.

Vision

Where do you see this business going after "x" number of years? What are your aspirations, and what's the next level of this business?

Goals

Here you'll list both your long-term and short-term goals. These should be realistic yet challenging goals. You'll also describe how you'll measure your performance using KPIs and your milestones.

Target Market

While you'll get into your target market in detail in the marketing plan section, an overview of your target market and its unique characteristics goes here.

Industry

What's the industry you're getting into, and what's its current state? Is it expanding, mature, or stable? What are the speculations for this industry in the short and long runs? Are there any gaps or opportunities you're utilizing? How are your competitors in this industry doing, and what's your edge over them?

Legal Structure

What kind of business will you be running? Will it be a sole proprietorship, an LLC, partnership, or corporation? Do you have any partners or investors holding some of your shares? How are the shares divided?

Products and Services

In this section you'll get into the details regarding your products and/or services. You should include the following:

1. A detailed description of your products and/or services. If there are any technical specification documents, attach them to the Appendices.
2. What problems do they solve? Explain in detail their benefits, features, and competitive advantage over similar products and services.
3. Are there any proprietary features backing up your competitive edge? This can be a patent, a license, or an exclusive agreement with one of your strategic partners that none of your competitors have.
4. What's the pricing strategy for your products and services? Will it be based on subscription, on one-time-pay, fees, or a lease? How does your pricing stand among the competition? What's your profit margin?

Marketing Plan

Your marketing plan covers the details about the industry, your competition, your target market, and your marketing strategy. You need to start with the following:

Market Research

In your market research, you'll get your information from two sources: data that you collect yourself, and the available data in journals, research articles, and trusted whitepapers. Through your research, you should acquire the following information:

- What's the total size of your industry?
- What's the industry outlook? Is it expanding or diminishing?
- The total size of your target market in the industry
- Realistically speaking, how much of this target market can you reach and/or dominate?
- What are the trends in your target market? What will your customers expect from you?

Obstacles

Are there any obstacles that will come in the way of your entering the market? How do you plan on overcoming them? These obstacles can be:

- High costs of starting up, production, marketing, or operation
- Strong competition
- Hiring employees of sufficient qualifications on a limited budget

Threats and Opportunities

Once you have a solid plan to overcome the barriers, what are the challenges you're going to face once you're in the industry? What are the opportunities you can use for your benefit? It's common to perform a SWOT analysis in this section of the plan.

Target Customers

You'll get into your target customers in detail in this part. You'll divide them into "user personas", listing the distinguishing characteristics of each one, their behaviors, and what would attract them to your products/services

Key Competitors

You've already given an overview of your competitors, and now it's time to get into more detail. You'll create a detailed competitor's data collection plan in which you'll include:

- Their prices

- Their benefits and features

- How profitable and scalable their business is

- Their marketing strategy

Next, you'll use this data to compare where you stand to them in a competitive analysis worksheet. This is where you list all your marketing aspects and compare it to theirs, ranking your performance to get a clear idea of where you stand in the market.

Positioning

Once you're clear about your industry, threats, opportunities, target customers, and key competitors, you should know how you'll position your business in the market using your competitive advantage.

Marketing Strategy

Your marketing strategy will include the online and offline portals you're going to use. If you focus on online marketing, you'll need to include the platforms you'll use, your content marketing strategy, your promotional strategy, and your PR plan.

Operational Plan

Your operational plan should give the reader a clear idea about your business's daily operations. To do that, you'll describe:

Production & Quality Control

What are the methods you'll use to produce a physical product or deliver an intangible service? If there are any equipment and/or technology costs, you should specify them in detail. You should also describe your plan on how you'll provide consistent quality in your products and services.

Location

If your business has a physical address, you should specify it in detail. This includes its complete address, the size of your office, the type of building, accessibility, facility costs, and utilities.

Legal Environment

Are there any legal requirements you should handle? These can include licenses, permits, insurance coverage, regulations, copyrights, or bonding.

Personnel

What kind of personnel will be working on your team? Will you hire full or part-timers? Freelancers or contractors? What's the job description, qualifications, and compensation of each? How will you find your team, and what sort of training will they need?

Other Operations

If your business depends on other operations, such as inventory maintenance, suppliers, or distribution channels, you should specify them in detail.

Management and Organization

This is where you describe the roles of everyone in your business. In describing your management team, you should include the following:

- Their biographies

- How you'll cover any gaps in the management structure

- Your business advisors

- An organizational chart

Expenses and Capitalization

These are the expenses you'll need to for launching. It doesn't include your daily finances, those will be included in your financial plan. For this section, you'll describe the following in detail:

- Your startup expenses

- Your launching day expenses

- Personal financial statement

Financial Plan

Your financial plan will cover in detail your daily expenses, projecting, in turn, your profit and growth over specified periods. In your financial plan, you'll discuss the following:

- Projection of profits and losses in first twelve months after startup

- A speculated balance sheet about the financial state of your business one year after launching
- An operational plan of three years that speculates your profits and losses
- The details of your cash flow at any given time

Appendices

You'll find that, across your plan, there are many detailed documents that serve the purpose of the section you're working on. However, whoever is reading your plan will most likely want to get an overview at first without getting into too many technical details. For this purpose, you'll include these documents in your Appendices.

Refining the Plan

Depending on the purpose of your plan, you might want to refine it to match whoever will be reading it. As we've mentioned previously, an investor will be looking for certain financial and strategic aspects of your business, but they might not want to know whether you intend to hire full-time employers or freelancers. Once you've finalized your plan, you'll be able to refine it to better match your purpose, maybe even create different versions for different targets.

Business Plans Best Practices

When it comes to business plans, there are way too many. They differ in many aspects, from the elements discussed to their layouts and styles of presentation. Here are some of the best practices when it comes to creating a business plan:

Data Visualization and Organization

If you look at this marketing strategy created by Nivea for Men, you'll find that they've used a simple diagram to convey their tactics.

Other forms of data visualization and organization can include diagrams, charts, and tables.

Trustworthy Resources

Sometimes getting accurate information can be difficult, no matter how much your business depends on the accuracy of this information. This is something that the managers at Airport Cafe were able to find their way around when they wanted to open a new branch in another terminal. They collected the data they needed about passengers and their behavior directly from the Airport Authorities, which allowed them to create a correct estimation in their business plan.

Concise Yet Comprehensive Information

A long business plan is not always the best; if you're able to address your key points in a shorter one, that will probably be best. This is a fictional concise-yet-comprehensive plan that serves its purpose:

How All Great Businesses Have Bulletproof Plans

If you're still having second thoughts about the importance of business plans, then perhaps you need to look at any of the successful businesses operating today and research their startup. They didn't start with getting finances, they didn't hire their team members first, and they most certainly didn't start with pitching their business idea. Their work started long before anyone had ever heard of them. It all started with a plan, a plan about what to do long before their business was ready to go out into the light, and a plan covering what they needed to do once their business was launched.

And yet, many people spend extraordinary amounts of time and effort creating a business plan, only to become discouraged and give up on their dream altogether. The reason is usually that when it finally comes time for execution, their business plan isn't executable; it isn't realistic. That shouldn't make you think that business plans are worthless; on the contrary, it should encourage you to bulletproof your plan.

The way great businesses bridge the gap between a business plan on paper and a successful real-life business is by putting everything they know on paper. Next, they research, talk to mentors, listen to the stories of those who've walked this path before, and then re-evaluate their plan. Perhaps the most important aspect of creating a bulletproof plan is, well, to bulletproof it. That can only happen by letting yourself go as far and high with your imagination, dreams, and aspirations as you want - and then grounding your plan with down-to-earth bulletproofing.

Chapter Three: Finances Sorted

Starting and running a business both require capital, which is often difficult to acquire. A crucial step towards a successful business involves birthing the finances for its operation. Anyone who has a great business idea and a plan to develop it can fall back when it comes to the financial aspect. Basic questions like, "How much will it cost me? Will I be able to gather enough capital? What if my plan backfires and I end up losing all my money?" are off-putting.

It is a big risk to put in a huge amount of money with the uncertainty of getting it back. But if you possess the drive and passion for getting your business where it deserves to be, you are bound to get the return of your investment and more. You just need a plan and a straight mind to set it up, which is what this book is about.

Getting your finances in order can be a complicated process, especially when you have just stepped into the business world. To ease the stress, we have divided this stage into various categories to help you understand all aspects in depth.

Let's begin by talking about the primary financial aspect of your funding plan: startup capital.

What is Startup Capital?

To earn money, you need money. It's the pragmatic truth behind every business. A company would require a certain amount of funding to begin running, which is known as startup funding or startup capital. This might include basic costs from purchasing equipment for your business to covering employee salaries and paying taxes.

There are certain varying terminologies depending on the type of capital you are approaching. For instance, the term seed capital refers to the funding required for planning and researching your idea before you finalize it. Startup capital is the funding required for the basic costs before launching, such as workspace rent and setup.

The next type is expansion capital, also known as mezzanine capital, which takes your company to a higher level and funds the improvements made for its growth.

There are a lot of ways to gather funding for your business, which we will cover in further detail. To understand it in a basic sense, capital is categorized as one of two types: debt capital and equity capital.

Debt Capital

This label applies to the capital borrowed either through banks or in the form of loans from relatives or lenders with interest rates and fees. Even though it takes a while to pay back the full amount with the additional costs, you would still be the sole owner of the company without sharing any equity or partnership.

Equity Capital

Equity capital is when an investor or a bigger company agrees to fund your business when it is in its initial stage in exchange for a certain percentage of the company's profits. It gives them the benefit of profiting from it when the business has grown and is running successfully. Even though you are relieved from repaying the loan amount, there is the forfeit of a stake in your company, affecting its functioning and negating sole ownership.

Funding Your Business – The Options

While there are multiple funding options, each comes with a set of benefits and risks. You need to weigh them out and decide on the most sensible one, or elect more than one option and garner funding from two or three sources, which could help reduce the risks of losing everything at once and provide a back-up plan in case of failure of one source.

A few finance options to fund your business are:

Savings or Self-Financing

The first plan would be to self-finance your business; it is relatively easy and less of a procedure to convert your personal assets into business capital. Having a personal investment in your business shows your commitment to the enterprise, which is a strong selling point for potential investors and business partners; it will not only get your business running sooner but could also attract extra funding.

There is a big downside to putting in a personal investment. If your business fails, you will end up losing everything, which will have a huge impact on your life. The fear of this may well provide you the motivation to work harder and make sure your business succeeds; if it does, you will recoup your investment and realize some profit that much earlier.

Taking a Loan

When you want to avoid the risk of losing all your savings and ending up nowhere, your backup plan would be taking a bank loan. It is, however, a nerve-wracking procedure given the amount of data and papers it requires. Moreover, the interest charged is anywhere from 6% to 14%, which adds up to a huge sum at the end. Getting a loan is not easy, because you're required to present either collateral of equivalent value to the mortgage it or an amazing credit score. A poor credit score/history means lessened odds of getting a loan, but there are banks and lenders who charge a higher interest rate while lending a small principal amount to the poor credit-score holders.

Another popular option is to enlist a co-signer on a loan; the co-signer can be a friend or relative who has a good credit score. In case of failure to repay, the bank will seek out the co-signer, so consider the implications if using this option.

Search for various lenders, talk to them, compare their services and interest rates, and go for the best.

Crowdfunding

Having recently gained considerable traction, crowdfunding is a popular choice among start-up companies who have their marketing strategies and product display ready to show to their audience. There are a lot of websites now which encourage and support crowdfunding. It is basically a platform where companies that have insufficient funds but a great idea pitch their concept to the general audience and request small contributions from the greatest possible number of them. It is sometimes accompanied by promises of discounted or free merchandise once the company is running.

These crowdfunding websites market themselves, so having your concept presented on them is a viable tool for attracting potential clients as well as investors. They will definitely cut themselves a small percentage of the gathered fund; however, be advised that if the crowd-funding website fails to collect the total anticipated amount, you do not get anything, and the money is returned to the respective donors. So, to receive large donations from a lot of individuals, you need to present a promising concept displayed impressively. Use creative ways to do so, like an animated video, a podcast, or a detailed presentation of your long-term goals.

Angel Investors

Angel investors are usually past owners of a successful business, or simply rich individuals who have a penchant for business and are ready to invest in potential business ideas. These angel investors often like to be a part of the company's accounting and management department, or an active member of the board of directors, using their control of the background activities to be more informed.

You don't need to have personal contacts to search for an angel investor. There are organizations that have advisory relationships with numerous angel investors that could support your business if intrigued by its concept.

Venture Capital

Also known as VC, Venture Capital firms look for start-up companies with stellar growth potential, or, sometimes, companies already established, and generally in the computer or high-tech fields.

Venture capitalists invest a huge amount of capital in businesses, expecting to gain equity stakes from their investments along with selling them as an IPO (initial public offering) or to other established businesses.

Venture Capital investment can provide significant capital for your business if it requires large funding, but the results delivered need to be exceptional. Venture capitalists expect not only a return of investment but also huge profits from your promising idea.

Borrowing from Friends and Family

If you want to avoid selling stakes from your business or paying usurious interest, borrowing money from your friends and family may be a viable option. Your family and friends understand that it takes time to build a business and that profits usually start coming in only after a few years; they might be inclined to give you a generous amount of time to return the borrowed money.

You might want to consider the risks of ruining relationships that come with this option. It would be difficult to pay them back in case your business fails, weakening their trust in you. At times, a few practical thinkers might want some kind of equity in your business as well, raising the chance of increasing complications between you. So, think twice before considering this option. It might be the easiest but it also comes with the most emotional risk.

Other Financing Options

Credit cards are another way to cover your initial expenses. The amount of money you borrow comes with a huge interest rate at the end of each month, which can get daunting. If you have used a credit card before, you probably know how quickly the interest adds up in case you neglect to repay in full. Certain credit-card deals, however, are tailored to meet business funding demands, providing cash-back and other attractive options.

Business incubators are an attractive option to receive additional services and advice, along with capital funding. They provide resources, tools, technical assistance, and/or marketing to save a new business money until the company can move into its own premises. Often, universities or some government organizations act as business incubators to benefit from the product development, marking them as an important section of the business forever. There are a few downsides to seeking a business incubator, such as going through a long procedure to get in, and higher chances of being rejected if there is too much competition or if your idea is not promising enough to succeed.

And then, there are **online peer-to-peer ("P2P") loan organizations** that lend money to small businesses with a straightforward approach unlike banks. You just fill in your request for funding and your business outline, and the website helps you receive the total fund from a pool of investors. You then need to repay the platform in monthly installments which go back to the investors. It also gives you lower interest rates and higher chances of approval. However, you need to have a good credit score to be considered for receiving funding. This approach of benefiting from P2P platforms is increasingly popular due to its ease of use and higher success rates.

If you have already sorted out the funding for your business's startup, there are further aspects that need to be managed while starting your company.

Budgeting and Upfront Costs

To start a business, a few basic costs are absolutely necessary and unavoidable. You need to budget to cover all costs for the first two to three years of starting your business. Forget about earning profit within this period. You need to solely focus on running the company smoothly without financial stress.

A few things to keep in mind while budgeting your start-up finances are:

-

Calculating the basic upfront costs required to start any kind of business. We have a checklist here which will help in managing those.

1. License and Registration Fees
2. Equipment and Tools such as computers, printers, billing machines, furniture, etc.
3. Office and Workspace Costs such as monthly rents or renovations
4. Insurance
5. Taxes
6. Employee Salaries
7. Product Development (depending on your business type)
8. Marketing and Advertising
9. Inventory
10. Website and Application Development
11. Utilities and Office Supplies
12. Miscellaneous costs such as hiring consultants, travel, or shipping

-

- Coming up with a realistic figure of how much money you can spend each month and dividing the costs accordingly, depending on the monthly expense and sales.

- Setting the total amount of funding you would require after these calculations and estimating the time duration you would need it for. Make sure to increase and decrease your sales graph calculations depending on the seasonal demand. Often, companies need a few years to get to the break-even point, and thus, a realistic time period would give you the chance of repaying the total investment amount within the promised time.

- Overestimating the budget and keeping an emergency fund on the side can help you cover unexpected costs such as equipment damage or covering employee salaries during sales lulls.

- Once you have your required amount along with the emergency fund, arranging for the total a few months in advance. Even if you are aiming to receive the needed amount through various options at once, approach them at the same time and make efforts to receive them all at once. This will let you start your company at a smoother pace.

Where Can You Cut Costs?

Money saved is money earned. Cutting costs while starting a business can help in saving a lot of money in unimaginable ways. These are a few tips through which you can cut costs:

- Look for numerous insurance policies and land on one which is cost-effective
-

- Reduce travel costs by conducting virtual meetings and interviews. It will also save you a lot of time which can be put into something more productive.

- Try purchasing supplies and utilities in bulk instead of smaller quantities. Buying them in bulk can get you a wholesale price instead of retail.

- If you have a basement or a warehouse that's been locked up and unused for a while, you can renovate it and use it as an office space. It will save you from paying rent every month, which is a major expense.

- If you feel that your workload doesn't require a full-time employee, you can hire fewer staff members and get particular tasks done by freelancers or virtual assistant companies, hence saving monthly salary payments.

Cutting costs to manage finances is an arduous phase in the beginning. However, skimping on necessary aspects, such as avoiding marketing or purchasing low-quality equipment, can affect the functionality of your business.

Common Mistakes and Pitfalls to Avoid

- Never underestimate your startup capital. You can incur unexpected costs at any point. Always overestimate your budget to be assured of meeting your monthly expenses.

- Avoid the mistake of expecting too much too soon. Being extremely optimistic about higher sales and timely payments can lead to improper budgeting of your finances every month. Sometimes, payments are delayed, or sales are decreased due to off-season fluctuations. You should

- be prepared to absorb the costs when you do not receive the expected returns.

- You cannot leave out your salary. Many entrepreneurs fail to add their own salaries on the balance sheet, even months after establishing their business, as a way of cutting costs. If you feel that your business cannot pay you well enough after a while, what's the point of running it in the first place?

- Do not take too many loans. It will just pile up your debt and affect your credit score in the longer run. If you are taking a loan to pay off the earlier one, you are just adding other fees and interests, making the situation worse for you. Arrange a proper refinancing plan and look for more sensible options to combat this situation.

To sum up the financial aspect of beginning your business, answer the following questions to come up with a rough idea about the direction you want to take:

- Which funding option seems the most feasible for you?

- Do you want to take a loan and repay the full amount within a few years?

- Are you ready to share a percentage of your company with an investor to receive the funding?

- Do you have a proper budgeting plan regarding the dollar amount and the time required to reach the break-even point?

-

- Can you support yourself until you make a profit?
- Are you ready to face unexpected financial situations? Do you have an emergency funding plan?
- Can you arrange for the total capital requirements well in advance?

Consider these questions honestly and realistically, because financing a business is not child's play. You must be thoroughly prepared and informed and take the leap only when you are fully confident of overcoming any circumstances.

Chapter Four: Finding A Mentor - Learn from the Experience of Others & Know Your Limits

Business publications and entrepreneurship books are great sources of the latest business news and strategies. The authors of these pieces are professionals who started from square one and are able to provide helpful insight to help you evaluate where you stand in your current plan, and how far you are from your goal. However, no matter how resourceful these online sources can be, they can never compare to hands-on mentorship from a business guru who can guide you on an on-going basis until your project is on a firm footing.

In short, a business mentor is a professional business owner who can act as your guide for an extended period, free of charge.

You might wonder why business gurus would want to invest their time and effort on new entrepreneurs if there is no financial compensation. For many of them, it's because they want to give back to their community and help mentees overcome the obstacles that the mentors once faced.

This section will guide you through the steps needed to find the right business mentor for your project, and how to maintain a long-lasting relationship with them that will help you and your business head in the right direction.

Why Get a Mentor?

While this isn't an obligatory step in growing your business, it will certainly accelerate the time taken to see your project boom. When you start your own business, you become your own boss, which can be challenging when you're still a budding entrepreneur. Having a mentor will speed up the sometimes-painful process of learning the intricacies of business implementation and leadership.

Getting Started: Where to Find a Mentor
Educate yourself first

While finding a mentor is an optional step, it's not one that you can leap to; never skip self-teaching. Make it a habit to read business publications and books; feed your own learning process and keep yourself updated on the latest news in commerce. Keep your mind business oriented.

Bear in mind that one day *you* may be the mentor, teaching a mentee who has reached out to you.

Explore local business communities and events

Whether it's a local Chamber of Commerce or informal business meetups in your area, such community events will often have entrepreneurs who are willing to give their insights to attendees. Even better, they will generally welcome being approached by less experienced individuals asking for mentorship

With that said, these kinds of meetups or workshops are a great place to meet *potential* mentors, but that doesn't mean that you should decide whom you want to establish as your coach on a whim. If you meet anyone whom you think can provide you with useful information, ask them anything off the top of your head in the meantime, and request their contact information to formally introduce yourself later and find out where you can meet them again.

Join a startup incubator

Incubators are tailored spaces for young entrepreneurs with limited funds or very few employees. These spaces have resources that help a growing business get started and overcome hurdles by providing a free or affordable workspace alongside access to investors and potential mentors. In some cases, incubators can even offer you capital and/or will recommend the right mentor for your business needs.

But you don't have to follow their recommendations; take time to explore the space and see if you spot any business owners that may provide you with insight into areas where you lack skills or need information. While recommended mentors may be a perfect fit for your business, they may not fit with *your* skills and needs.

Use your own connections

While exploring beyond the parapet of your former connections is an excellent way to broaden your professional network, never underestimate the power of professionals who once inspired you in the past. These could be business owners with whom you crossed paths years ago, or college professors who know the convolutions of the business world best and likely know more about your field of choice than your peers.

If you're unsure how to determine whether a professional could be of help, ask yourself if they have a broad network of business gurus and investors from which to draw their information. Some of them may not have the time to mentor, but others will be willing to provide you with what you need to further your career.

How to Choose a Mentor

Never choose an investor to be your mentor

Your circle of investors and peers are trusted individuals who want your project to succeed as much as you do, and that's exactly why they cannot provide you mentorship. Anyone, including friends or family, who might be emotionally invested in you or your project, should never be those you turn to for critique.

Advice should never be sugarcoated, and sometimes getting feedback will be as harsh as a professional frankly telling you that your business model is not feasible or that it's unlikely to succeed. These are insights that a friend or investor will never be able to perceive because they're typically thinking inside the same box as you.

An ideal business mentor is someone who can see the full picture and whose relationship with you is strictly professional. This doesn't mean that you need someone who will give you nothing but negative feedback, but mentors should be honest and analytical as well as motivating. Quality mentorship should always have a positive effect on entrepreneurs, driving them to dream big and take long shots but through realistic strategies.

Choose a good listener

A professional who doesn't take the time to listen to you and only throws generic advice your way is a bad fit for you, and in most cases, for any other entrepreneur as well. You've already had your share of general How-To's and technical advice from books and business news. What you should be looking for is someone who will answer *your* questions, rather than provide you with a set of generic FAQs.

A good listener will take your personal struggles into account and generously offer advice on each of your inquiries. Some of them will take the time to listen to what you have to say all at one go, in order to analyze your character and see what approaches could work for you.

A mentor should never assume that you will be making the same decisions that they would. Instead, they should think like the best version they believe you could be, rather than the best version of themselves.

Choose a humble mentor

Mentors should never be parental or condescending. Although the latter is uncommon, you'll find yourself running into the former quite often on your hunt for the perfect mentor. A good mentor will treat you as their equal, and not as a child that reminds them of their earlier days. Oddly enough, this is more common among younger successful entrepreneurs who have recently "made it."

A mentor should never treat you like they're your boss; one of the primary reasons you've decided on this journey is to be your own boss. Professionals who make good mentors will offer you advice, not orders. They will recommend trying out certain strategies, but will not assign you homework. Someone who behaves as your superior will gradually cause you to feel dependent on receiving orders, when it's essential for you to feel confident that you can take the wheel once your mentor is no longer in the picture.

Don't be afraid to go big

Do not purposely aim for a smaller target-mentor, assuming that more prestigious business owners will not agree to be your mentor. On the contrary, established companies are *more* likely to have CEOs that dedicate a good chunk of their time to give back to the community.

That doesn't mean that only famous entrepreneurs will have the qualities that render them the quintessential mentor. Even those who run relatively small businesses can be of immense help. If you come across a business that it inspires you, large or small, never hesitate to try to meet the mastermind behind it.

Connecting: How to Set Up Meetings
Make yourself reachable

Once you've met your mentor, you need to make yourself easily accessible to them. Always return their calls and respond to their emails as swiftly as possible. A mentor should never have to chase you for a meeting from which *you* will benefit.

Be frank with your mentor about what you expect

Avoid using the word "mentor" in your first meeting. Even though they probably expect it, you should take the time to connect in those first casual meetings, discussing your common interests and insights in the business world. The first meeting will allow both of you to decide whether the other person is a good fit for a mentoring relationship.

As you follow up with them, you may then bring up your interest in mentorship and regular consultation. If they agree to your proposition and offer a fee, turn it down. An entrepreneur should never have to pay for mentorship.

Invest in your relationship

Once you have established your mentor-mentee relationship, make sure you frequently meet up. The whole purpose of mentorship is to learn what textbooks can't teach you: hands-on experience. It would be a waste of a connection to rely on back-and-forth emails between you and your mentor.

Take them to your workspace or office. Discuss your concerns and any hurdles in the way of your business growth, and introduce your mentor to your personnel, if you have any.

Business Mentorship: What to Expect

Honest feedback

What to expect from your mentor is primarily something that *you* decide, unless your business growth is stunted for reasons that you don't understand or can't pinpoint. If you've picked the right mentor, they will start by offering you an all-encompassing evaluation of your business idea, model, and how effectively you're running your company.

Many entrepreneurs are so emotionally invested in their business models and ideas that they typically reject any critique, and only want a series of crash courses. This will never be the case. Be emotionally prepared for critique and listen to your mentor's advice on how to improve areas that need some work.

A personal approach

A business mentor will confidentially listen to your concerns and analyze everything that worries you about your business. They will not provide you psychiatric counseling, nor will they only give you technical advice. They're not business advisors, they're confidantes. Expect them to share their own stories of failure and how they managed to overcome the drawbacks. They may pinpoint your weaknesses and advise you on how to work on them.

Help you didn't expect

Let's say that the primary reason you consulted a mentor was that you were looking to implement an impeccable sales model. You may find that your mentor will stop you and take you two steps back, to where you missed something more important. They may point out poor time management skills, ask you about your sleeping habits, advise you to give yourself more time off, and provide you with other advice that you least expected.

And even though it may feel like there's no time to slow down, your mentor speaks of experience and knows best when it comes to a healthy working pace. You may think that working upwards of ten hours a day will get you to launch your business faster, but your mentor knows that it will end up burning you out in a matter of weeks, leading to further delay. Listen to your mentor and learn from their failures and experiences.

EQ skills

You can't have a successful business with unhappy employees. Your mentor should teach you to have better control over your own emotions as well as that of your personnel. They will work on making you more self-aware of your weaknesses and strengths. They'll also advise you on how to interact with your employees in a manner that is motivational while maintaining boundaries that will have your personnel seeing you as a supportive superior.

During your mentorship, you should feel your motivation become more grounded in realistic goals. Your mentor will help you understand that while dreaming big is helpful, baby steps should be applied wherever possible.

Mentorship is an efficient way to make sure you're on the right track, but it's not a delegation of responsibilities. A mentee primarily does all the work, while a mentor will find ways around weaknesses, and will make sure that no risky decisions are made without the consequences being pointed out to their mentees. Remember that you're not taking a shortcut by consulting another professional, but rather, you're learning from the hands-on experience of other business gurus to up your chances of success.

Chapter Five: The Company You Keep - Who Is Going on The Journey with You?

Two heads are better than one when it comes to running a business and finding the right partner for your journey can generate significantly more great ideas and solutions to problems. It's also good security to have someone to rely on in the event you have to opt-out temporarily, while having more shoulders to bear responsibilities.

When it comes to startups, a partner can help lower the costs to launch by providing more capital. You may think that splitting the income sounds less appealing, but in most cases, the benefits outweigh the costs.

But finding the right partner for your startup is a tricky business, and it doesn't just boil down to someone you can trust with your company. Although having a partner can open more doors for your business, you're also looking at twice as many disagreements, legal liabilities, weaknesses, and other changes that may threaten the success of your project.

Before you consider finding a business partner, let's look at how you could avoid a detrimental partnership by considering these areas.

What Makes a Business Partnership Detrimental?

An efficient way to make sure that you don't get caught up in a bad partnership is to know what *makes* a partnership bad. These are some of the most common signs that indicate a detrimental business alliance.

Responsibilities are unbalanced

Labor and supervision should always be equally divided based on each partner's strengths and weaknesses. If you're a particularly creative individual, but you lack in marketing knowledge, for instance, a good partner is one who will bear the brunt of marketing management while allowing you to exercise a greater role in R&D.

Aside from capital and startup funding, dividing labor is the primary reason why many companies opt for partnership. So, before any contracts are signed, make sure that you divide tasks beforehand to make it clear what each of you should expect.

Communication is difficult

Neither partner should make any decisions of serious consequence without consulting the other. The two of you should be able to frequently communicate in person, or at least through emails, to stay in the loop of the happenings on the other side of the boat. If your partner takes a long time to respond to any inquiries or tends to prioritize their own opinions and decisions over yours, this is a red flag that should not be ignored.

There is a significant gap in experience level

The two previous points are oftentimes a result of one partner having more or less experience than the other. Of course, there is no accurate way to measure one's professional experience, but picking someone substantially older than you, and one who has been in the industry for much longer, may result in them taking your views less seriously.

On the other hand, someone who is less experienced may lack the confidence to take any initiatives, which will have you carrying the burden of all business obligations on your own shoulders.

Either of you is unable to compromise

A good business partner is one who could sacrifice an idea that they're emotionally attached to, in the event the second partner disagrees with its efficacy. Misunderstandings between partners are common and cannot be avoided; however, both of you should know how to compromise when you reach a fork in the road.

In that case, partners should put their own interests aside and consider what would be best for the company. Evaluate the decisions in question by pragmatically establishing the pros and cons of each. That way, one or both of you can compromise on your idea for the benefit of the company.

How Do I Find the Right Partner?

You may be surprised to know that the perfect partner for you and your business does not have to understand the intricacies of running a business impeccably. Instead, a partner is someone who can take realistic approaches to help contribute to company growth in one or more areas. Before you decide on a person to trust, ask yourself these questions.

Do we share a vision?

One of the reasons why it's smart to avoid drastically more experienced partners is because they will likely have different goals and an overall philosophy that contradicts yours. Ask your prospective partner where they see the company in several years, and what demographic they expect to cater to. It's crucial to find a partner who does not plan to change the core of your business.

Do we share the same skills?

If the answer is yes, it's time for you to browse other options. It's natural for you to be inclined to find someone as skilled as you are, but those skills should never be the same. It's a bad idea for partners to manage the same department because this could lead to countless disagreements. Instead, choose someone who could manage the departments you're least interested in running (based on lack of skill).

Is my partner confident?

It's not uncommon to find someone whose expertise in a certain field makes them a perfect fit for your company. However, ideas and long-term plans would be for naught if the person in charge is not confident enough to execute them or lead a team that can. Always choose someone confident of their own abilities, yet who has a realistic view of how far their skills can go.

Are There any Legal Measures I Should take Before Partnering?

The short answer is yes. Even if you choose someone whom you have known for years and know you can trust, there is a staple of legal measures that must be taken care of before you sign that partnership agreement.

Authorization of Managerial Decisions

If you don't have a clear list in your partnership agreement that determines what each of you is authorized to do on behalf of the company, the best-case scenario is that your favorite employee gets fired. The worst-case scenario? *You* get fired.

That's right. There have been numerous cases of partners being fired from their own companies by other shareholders. Even Steve Jobs was once fired from his own company after a disagreement with his CEO! Discuss with your lawyer how to incorporate a strict employee-owned policy in your contract.

Percentage of Ownership

You and your partner should always discuss beforehand how much each of you is willing to invest. More funds are not always better, as this will also alter the percentage of your ownership, which also decreases your income.

If it's a small business, you should never opt for more than one partner, and typically one who will contribute a share of less than half. More profit for you means that you can choose to invest more in the business to help it grow in the future, whereas your partner may not be willing to do the same.

Dissolution

If there's anything specific you're worried that your partner may do or refuse to do in the future, all of it should be included in the dissolution section of your contract. This means that your partnership can be *dissolved* or terminated in the event your partner overrides predetermined policies. This could include retirement, sharing confidential information, a change in profit sharing ratio, or simply the expiration of the agreement signed.

How Can a Partnership Go Wrong?

There are many more dangerous risks to consider if you choose to get a business partner, and they are not as simple as miscommunication and having to compromise. In fact, the following reasons are precisely why many startup founders decide against partnership altogether, no matter how much they may need the funds.

Limited Control

The Issue

You're not hiring a manager that you can let go if things don't go your way. An employed shareholder has full control over the division they run, which means that your hands will be tied if you disagree with the way they run their department. Partners *own* the company, too, and they *can* legally take risky decisions on the company's behalf without your knowledge. Of course, you could always add a policy in your agreement that would prevent such blatant behavior, but it's not as simple as that.

Or rather, sometimes, it IS much simpler than that, in that you have no legal way to prevent it. If you don't like how your partner treats employees, for instance, this is not something that could be prevented with a policy in a contract. And while partners may not be able to make big, impactful decisions without your approval, they still have full control over their designated department, which can go downhill if their strategies are faulty.

How to Prevent It

If you think you have the skills to run the company on your own but lack the funds, always opt for a silent partner, who has no say in operational matters and can only contribute to the company via capital. In return, they get their agreed share of the profit.

Loss of a Relationship

The Issue

While your handy business book may not include this risk in the partnership section, you need to understand that you're legally binding yourself to work hand-in-hand with a person for as long as your contract will last – which is, in some cases, forever. If you decide to make your spouse a partner, for instance, this will make the work environment less appealing to you if you ever part ways. Because unlike marriage, you cannot divorce your way out of a business partnership (dissolution notwithstanding).

That said, partnerships may also *lead* to breaking bonds between people. If you choose a friend or family as your partner, the common disagreements that both of you will have to deal with will inevitably impact how you view one another, and in many cases, it can be a cause of losing friends and disliking family members.

How to Prevent It

Avoid making old friends, spouses, or family your business partners, unless it's absolutely necessary. If you have limited options, avoid partnering with someone who can "retaliate" in the business place in the event you grow to be on bad terms in your personal life. For instance, a former spouse is more likely to wreak havoc on your work environment's peace in passive-aggressive ways than a parent or a sibling.

Legal Liability

The Issue

Picture this: it's been a few good years, and your company is seemingly doing great. You check your mail as you have your morning coffee, and you find an envelope with the civil court stamp. You read the letter and spit out your coffee as you read that you have been sued.

Your business partner can cause you to end up in court if they make a corporate decision that violates the law. Lawsuits can be extremely expensive, to the point that they can bankrupt a company. Just because *you* have no say in or knowledge of a small decision doesn't mean you won't be deemed accountable if it violates the law.

How to Prevent It

Partners must make sure that they both understand applicable laws, which in turn can be a burden. You'll feel the need to consistently monitor divisions for which you got a partner to alleviate the need for monitoring. It's pretty counterproductive and can add to the stress of having to run the company, but it is necessary to make sure your company is not executing anything illegal.

Reputation Risks

The Issue

Having your reputation on the line is one of the many risks that your lawyer can't help you with when signing the agreement. How your partner behaves within the company and in their personal life can and will impact your reputation.

How could their personal life affect the reputation of your company? Mostly through social media. It's not uncommon to hear of "cancel culture" putting a company out of business when a founder or partner expresses a bigoted opinion or says something that appalls the public. This is more common with bigger corporations, but you should never underestimate the power of word-of-mouth, even if you have a small business.

How to Prevent It

While it's advised to partner with someone in whom you're not too emotionally invested, your partner shouldn't be a complete stranger, either. Make sure you're aware of this person's views, how they act in stressful situations, and how far you could trust them with your business.

Are There any Other Disadvantages?

Aside from hefty risks, there may be some unpleasant disadvantages of partnership, even when matters go as planned.

Loss of Your Autonomy

So, you've invested every penny you own in a business and worked long and hard so you could make it to the top of the corporate ladder. Having a partner can make operational and financial matters easier, but it also means that you're not fully in charge of the company you worked so hard to start.

Obligatory Business Consent

A general partnership will prevent you from making any monumental operational decisions without the consent of your partner. This may become stressful for many founders, as they always, at heart, see the company as their own, regardless of partners.

Potential Failure in Case of Dissolution

Dissolution doesn't always happen when a partner is shady or dishonest. Sometimes they're obligatory in cases of death or withdrawal. If dissolution occurs when you least expect it, this can make your company financially or operationally unstable.

Why Should I Get a Partnership?

All the previous sub-sections may have covered reasons why you wouldn't want to invest in a partnership, but there are also many benefits if you choose the right partner.

Higher Capital

While the company's income is divided, your partner may have their own network of connections that could help make your company thrive and attract more customers. Having a partner also makes it easier for you to borrow capital to start your business, as this can make your lender evaluate a higher potential profit.

Work/Life Balance

It's not just the extra cash that makes partnerships worthwhile. It's the extra free time you get on your hands when you have someone that has your back. Partners also make it easier to take long vacations, as they can take over when you can't, and you get to return the favor. This will make sure that your company is in good hands when you're away for leisure or emergencies.

Wide Range of Expertise

You could be great at coming up with ideas, but not very good at marketing them. Or perhaps, you want to take over the finances of your company for security reasons, but you don't have the skill for it. Finding a partner who can fill in where you're lacking will multiply your company's chances of success.

Finding a business partner for your company is tricky and cannot guarantee the growth of your business. While it's an efficient way to divide responsibilities, potential risks may outweigh the benefits to some founders. If you need a partner to help you with funding, consider finding a silent partner.

Chapter Six: The Legal Status of Your Business Now and In the Future

When starting a business, choosing the legal business category you want your company to fall under affects how you make income, hire staff, and implement marketing strategies. In other words, that small decision of choosing what document you and your potential co-founders will sign will impact the future of your business. It's not a decision that should be taken lightly or on a whim, and it's best that you fully understand the nature of each type of business entity before you start your business.

That said, choosing the right business entity for your company doesn't mark the end of your legal responsibilities. A myriad of other steps and precautions need to be taken, such as preparing for taxes, potential liabilities, licensing, and any needed permits.

While this section will never replace a lawyer, it will allow you to predict the legal stages of starting a business and will acquaint you with everything expected of you from the legal authorities as a business owner. This guide will also help prepare you for legal complications that you may encounter in the future and help you to avoid or deal with them accordingly.

Entity Types

This sole decision determines the amount of taxes you pay, the loans you could be granted from investors, and your risk exposure in the event your company is sued. Although in most countries, there are tens of business-entity types to choose from, startups generally have the following six options:

Sole Proprietorship

If you don't have any partners or co-founders, a sole proprietorship is a simple, easy-to start business entity that documents you as the sole operator and owner of your business. What makes this entity easy for beginner entrepreneurs is that no corporate formalities need to be documented. Meaning, you won't be compelled to keep track of meeting minutes or other similar reports to pass an audit. Plus, you get to cut your business losses from your tax return.

However, this may not be in your best interest if the business will require hefty funding or loans, seeing as this will make you legally liable for all responsibilities. If your business is sued in the future, this can result in many of your assets being taken away from you as compensation. It may also be more challenging for you to get a business loan because there's little to no legal difference between you as a person and your business. The good news is, you can eventually convert your sole proprietorship company into an LLC or corporation when your business thrives.

General Partnership (GP)

If your company has more than a single owner, your most viable option will likely be a GP entity. This will allow all partners to manage the business and divide profits and losses accordingly. Just like its sole-proprietorship counterpart, you won't be required to register for it, and paperwork is fairly easy. GP entities are just as easy to start; however, the upside is, you won't have to be liable for funding arrangements and debts on your own.

Unless you sign a partnership agreement, this entity may be at risk of failure if disputes between partners do not reach a resolution. It's just as challenging as its sole-partner counterpart to get loans from investors, seeing as your entity is not registered. For early businesses with lower funding, this may be the ideal option, as partners can share liabilities until they can convert their business into another entity type.

Limited Partnership (LP)

While this business entity is not as easy to start, being registered makes it safer and gives your company more options when it comes to funding and finding investors. Paperwork must be filed with the state, and you must document yourself as an active partner, or a general partner, and others as limited partners, also known as silent partners.

Silent partners have no control over how you operate your company but invest in your business in return for an agreed-upon share of the profit determined by their ownership percentage. This business option makes it easier to raise money, as your investors can identify as limited partners and will not be personally liable for any legal issues that your company may face. That said, this entity is far more expensive to start, primarily because it requires a state filing.

It's possible for general partners to avoid personal liability from their peers' actions through a limited-liability partnership (LLP); however, most countries and states only grant this entity to law and accounting firms and doctor's offices.

C-Corporation

C-corps are possibly the most appealing entities to startups and will open doors to various sources of funding for your company, but they're also one of the most challenging and expensive entities to start. C-corps are independent and separate from a company's owner and are also shareholders in the business. So, you have a board of officers and directors running the company (the owners), and investors who fund the project. What makes it appealing is that the owners are not legally liable for any debts or litigation-related liabilities.

This type of entity is also eligible for more tax deductions than any other entity, as the owners pay lower taxes as self-employers.

That said, filing fees are more expensive, and while the company is initially eligible for tax cuts, it also regularly faces double taxation – shareholders tax and corporate tax. Also, shareholders are unable to deduct any business losses on tax returns.

S-Corporation

S-corps are similar to C-corps but have the added benefit of being a pass-through entity, meaning tax returns and deductions are more practical. Through this entity, shareholders are not legally liable for debts, while the corporation's losses are made up for through tax returns. An S-corp does not face double taxation or corporate taxation.

However, for obvious reasons, they're very expensive to start and pose more limits on investing options when it comes to issuing stock.

Limited Liability Company (LLP)

To put it in colloquial terms, LLPs give you the best of both worlds when it comes to liabilities and profit. But as previously mentioned, only a few services are eligible for this entity type, and even then, they may run into more difficulties when it comes to gathering the funds needed to register the company.

LLP companies have fewer paperwork requirements; they essentially operate like sole proprietorships and partnerships, but with added benefits. You have the choice to have the IRS deem you a pass-through entity or a corporation, based on how you want to be taxed. On top of that, corporate formalities are not as strict as those required to run S-corps or C-corps.

When you decide on a business structure, you need to bear in mind that there are other legal requirements that need to be taken care of to ensure that your business will operate smoothly with all the right permits, licensing, and tax preparation methods. Here's what you may need to know.

What Permits and Licenses Do I Need?

This stage of getting your startup on its feet is one of those phases that will have you rushing from one office to the other to get the needed documents. And although there's no way to avoid making this stage tedious, it helps to know the requirements are based on what your business does. Not all these permits or licenses will be required; it all depends on the work environment of your business, and what your product or service involves in the production and management processes.

General Business License

This license essentially registers your business for taxation. Businesses in general are required to have a general business license issued by the city or state. You should expect an inspection of your workplace for an evaluation of public safety and social impact.

This license will also be helpful if your business requires buying wholesale goods, as it will negate additional sales tax.

Fire Department Permit

If your company uses flammable materials, you're going to need a permit from your fire department. This is one of those permits that you must get before opening your business to the public. In some areas, you may not be required to have a permit, but will have periodic inspects that evaluate the safety of your work environment. If you don't meet the safety regulations, a citation will be issued. Any crowded, closed spaces such as daycares or restaurants are subject to these inspections.

Environmental Permit

Although this doesn't apply to all cities, many now have environmental protection offices that work to limit air and water pollution. If your industry burns any materials or disposes any liquids into sewers, a permit is likely needed. If you don't know if you have any environment offices in your city, quick research or a phone call to your lawyer may be of help.

Sign Permit

It usually never crosses an entrepreneur's mind when they place a sign right outside their new working space that they might be doing something against the law. Some cities have regulations when it comes to sign size and location; check your city's regulations, and have your landlord sign their approval before you hang that sign on your office door.

Zoning Permit

A zoning permit determines where your business can and cannot operate, and this also includes home business owners. Depending on your service or product, you may be subject to operating only in certain areas. However, you can counter this by applying for a variance or what's also known as a conditional-use permit to operate in the area which is not zoned for your business.

Professional License

Although the requirements vary according to the city or state in which you wish to operate, professional licenses may be required. This applies to special services ranging from hairdressing to childcare. Professions like accounting will also be required to acquire special licenses.

Construction Permit

If, for any reason, you are rebuilding or altering the construction of your workplace, you will have to obtain a construction permit before you make any alterations.

Federal License

Your business may need a license from a federal agency if it involves activities like manufacturing or selling alcohol or firearms. You'll also need this license for activities related to wildlife, especially those that import or export animals.

Special State License

If you own a restaurant or any other establishment that deals with or serves alcohol to the public, your business will need a special license before it can operate, in order for the state to make sure that your service runs according to specific state standards and regulations. Failing to obtain this license and proceeding with your business may risk shutting it down.

Sales Tax Permit

If your company operates by selling goods, in person or online, your city or state will have to collect sales tax. In that case, a business permit will also be required, which is also known as a seller's permit. It's not as simple as it may seem, as there's a fine line between a service and a product, and oftentimes a service-provider may be required to pay sales tax as well.

What taxes will I have to pay?

Taxes are, unfortunately, not as simple as calculating a percentage of your profit, because there's a convoluted set of different federal, state, and local policies used to assess them. With that said, here are some of the challenges you may face when it comes to tax preparation.

Payroll and Taxes

Each shareholder in a company will be subject to personal taxes on the income they receive, which means that the business in question will have to file federal and state withholding taxes. It gets a little more complicated when you deduct taxes from your employees' paychecks. There are payroll services that make those calculations on your behalf, but startups may find they're paying more for the services than they are in taxes.

If you have employees other than company partners, you must pay worker's compensation and/or insurance, but only if you have more than three full-time employees.

License Fees

Other fees may include an annual sum that you pay if your business is registered with the State Corporation Commission. Any license you have registered for may be subject to an annual fee, so make sure you check your state's regulations to make sure your licenses stay in effect.

Business Structure

The primary factor that decides the taxes you're liable for is the business entity you have chosen for your company. Therefore, it's advisable to opt for limited liability or S-corp structures, as they will protect you from lawsuits and will provide you with plenty of tax advantages and returns. But since it all depends on the kind of service or product your company has to offer, it's best to consult an attorney for in-depth details.

Are There Other Legal Liabilities I Should be Aware Of?

A startup will have to be able to navigate a path of liability roadblocks before they're able to fully operate, which is why it's best to make a checklist of everything you may need to take care of before you launch your startup. These are additional legalities you will likely encounter.

Intellectual property protections

You're going to want to initiate copyrights and trademarks to protect your product from being copied. If you don't get these protections, you might have to face some very costly legal battles with your rivals. These kinds of protections also enhance the commercial value of your company and make it more appealing for both investors and customers. Suppliers, partners, and investors usually like to perform intellectual property checks before they make any agreements with you.

Non-disclosure agreements

These agreements constitute confidential information that may not be disclosed to other parties without the consent of all partners involved in a business. These also determine who owns said information, how long the information should be kept confidential, and how it should be handled. Non-disclosure agreements are issued to contractors, employees, and other third parties to ensure that your confidential business data stays confidential.

Employee contracts

Even startups at their earliest stages will need some employees, even if they're only involved part-time. You're going to have to legally bind them to a contract to protect their rights as well as yours. Many founders hire attorneys to take care of such documentation processes for them. A legal counselor is advised when signing contracts with executives, as some detrimental risks may be incurred if the contract is not drafted properly.

Privacy policies

A startup founder is responsible for managing privacy-policy protections. You will need to make matters transparent when it comes to data usage so that consumers know what they're dealing with and can learn to trust your service or the product you have to offer. These protections don't just make your business more appealing to the public, they also help bulletproof confidential user data from being breached.

Because these steps and precautious may differ depending on where you live, it's important to do some research on your industry and country or state. This guide should cover the legal liabilities you might be subject to, but they cannot replace a legal advisor or an attorney.

Chapter Seven: Your Business Is Born; Naming, Registering, And Insuring Your Business

This section will discuss the naming and registering of your company with the various government entities involved. It will also address how to protect your business by examining the various types of insurance available.

Choosing the company name is as fun as any creative endeavor can be. A lot will enter in to choosing the name.; it isn't just a matter of finding something that resonates with your brand identity, which is obviously still important. Your choice for a business name should take into consideration the fact that it must be unique and not currently in use by another entity.

Naming Your Business

Step 1: Check If the Chosen Name Is Available — Your Entity Name

Your entity name protects you at a state level. For example, if you named your company XYZ, there could exist another company with the exact same name in another state. So, if you have a name in mind, the first step would be to check if it is taken. There are a number of websites that will offer a free check, as well as government-operated websites that will do this specific to the state in which you will register your company.

The entity name is how your company will be legally identified by your state. Different states will have different rules, regulations, and procedures on how to register the name. Some states will even dictate that the company name must reflect the kind of business in which your company will engage. It is highly recommended to check state websites regarding their regulations.

Step 2: Do You Want or Need a Trademark?

The name you chose in step 1 does not protect your company's name outside your state. This means if you want to heavily brand your company and ensure no confusion between yourself and other legal entities, it may be wise to register your company name as a trademark. Trademarks protect you at a federal — national— level. Trademarks can be used for both your company and for goods or services. This comes in handy if your chosen name is desired by competitors in the same or similar industry.

As great as this security may be, it can be a double-edged sword. Infringing on someone else's trademark can prove costly if taken to litigation. The United States Patent and Trademark Office provides a database to check to see if your name, or product, or service names are already used. Follow this link: https://www.uspto.gov/trademark

Step 3: Consider a DBA Name

A DBA (Doing Business As) name is sometimes not required by your state laws but can prove to be beneficial for your company. A DBA may be commonly referred to as a fictitious name, trade name, or assumed name. This oftentimes comes handy if your company handles activity in different business sectors or wants to operate under different names but for the same company. To illustrate this, let's examine a company that owns and operates hotels. This company can have a name like XYZ and can own a hotel like a Hilton franchise, for example. The company could have a legal entity name of XYZ and do business as Hilton Franchise Hotel if that was their registered DBA.

This comes in handy for doing business with a more common name than your registered entity name; multiple people or business can operate with the same DBA in one state.

As with trademarks, filing for a DBA comes with a different ruleset from state to state, and you must consult government offices and websites for the state-specific procedures. Moreover, the rules for a DBA may vary depending on the county and municipality, or even depending on the company structure.

Step 4: Choosing a Domain Name

With the importance of having an online presence in today's market, your domain name is just as important to your company's success as your entity name. A domain name is the same as your website address.

Like your entity name, your domain name must be unique. But this extends beyond the state limitations on entity names, as domain names are worldwide. You must register your domain name through a registrar service. Here is a link to a directory of accredited registrar services: https://www.internic.net/regist.html

Please note that this registrar service is different from the domain-hosting services that actually host your website for you. However, most domain-hosting services will also register your domain name for you. Domain hosts will also explain the WHOIS registry, and how you can protect your company's privacy when registering your domain name.

Registering Your Business

With your names picked out and their availability verified, it is time to make it official and register the company with the government. This can be a multistep process that can be examined at two different levels; federal and state.

Federal Registration

Federal registration is not always necessary, depending on your company's legal structure. For example, if you have set up an S Corp, you will need to file form 2553 with the IRS (Internal Revenue Service).

Most businesses will not actually need to register federally to become a legal entity. But at the bare minimum, your business will apply for a federal tax ID number. This ID number is often referred to as an EIN (Employer Identification Number). An EIN is similar to a TIN (Taxpayer Identification Number) or SSN (Social Security Number) but is for a legal entity as opposed to an individual.

To apply for an EIN, follow the steps below:

- Visit: https://sa.www4.irs.gov/modiein/individual/index.jsp
- Click on Start Application
- Choose the type of company you have and click continue
- Read the information given then click on continue

The process will vary slightly depending on the selections you have made thus far, but as you navigate the website, the information will be provided and explained. Required forms will be available as links to PDF files. At the conclusion of the online procedure, your application for an EIN will be submitted. Remember to fill out the requested information accurately and factually. Oftentimes the website will check some of the information provided, such as your name and SSN, against existing IRS records. Errors here will slow down the completion of this process or may result in the rejection of the application.

More information on how to obtain an EIN can be found on the U.S. Small Business Administration website at the following link:

https://www.sba.gov/business-guide/launch-your-business/get-federal-state-tax-id-numbers.

State Registration

Most likely, you will need to register your company with your state. The scenarios where you are exempt from this are very limited; for example, if you operate under your personal name and have no form of liability protection. In the case of setting up your company as an LLC, corporation, partnership, or nonprofit corporation, you need to register with any state in which you conduct business activity. The extent at which you conduct business in a state resulting in the need for registration involves:

- Your business having a physical presence in the state
- Having frequent in-person meetings with clients or businesses in the state
- Your company's revenue is primarily or heavily contributed to by business in the state
- Any of your employees work in the state

How you register with the state will vary depending on the state. Depending on your state, you may be able to register online, but many states require you to file paper documents, either in person or through the mail. Most states will require you to register with the Secretary of State's office, a Business Bureau, or a Business Agency.

Getting a Registered Agent

If your company is an LLC, corporation, partnership, or nonprofit corporation, you need a registered agent. A registered agent receives official papers and legal documents on behalf of your company. You can list yourself for the role or discuss having your CPA (Certified Personal Accountant) or legal counsel being listed in your place.

State Filing Documents and Fees

Now that you have the information for filing, you need to actually do it. In other words, let's put all the information down on the forms and give them to the government to formally establish your company. As with most government procedures, this will cost money. While the cost for filing varies from state to state, it will generally cost under $300.

The forms you will fill out will ask for your business name and its location, ownership, management structure, or directors, the number and value of shares, and the registered agent information.

The documents you need will differ depending on your company structure.

LLCs will require Articles of Organization and an Operating Agreement, which are, respectively, a document describing the basics of your LLC and a document that describes your company's operations. The operating agreement defines the financial structure and members' roles, duties, powers, and responsibilities. Even if not required by the state, it is strongly recommended you create an agreement for your LLC. Some standardized LLC operating agreements are available for purchase, but you should consider having a qualified attorney draft a personalized agreement for your company.

LPs (Limited Partnerships) and LLPs (Limited Liability Partnerships) will require a certificate of limited partnership and certificate of limited liability partnership, respectively, which are simple documents that describe the basic partnership information to the state. You will also need a limited partnership agreement or limited liability partnership agreement, respectively. This is similar to the LLC operating agreement but created for a partnership as opposed to an LLC. Again, it is recommended you have a qualified attorney create this document.

Corporations will need articles of incorporation and bylaws or resolutions. Articles of incorporation are a comprehensive legal document that lays out the basic outline of your business. The most common information found on the articles of incorporation is the company name, business purpose or scope, number of shares offered, value of said shares, directors, and officers. The corporation bylaws are similar to the operating agreement an LLC would have but structured for a corporation's governance.

To access the required forms or websites, go to your states' Secretary of State website. The following link to the US Small Business Administration will ask you to select the state in which you are setting up your company, and then provide you with links to the relevant website.

https://www.sba.gov/business-guide/launch-your-business/register-your-business.

Don't worry if this a lot to digest; it's a lot of business lingo for new business owners, but it's all relatively simple in practice, and you are just filling out forms to establish your company. Your CPA or lawyer can carry out this process for you, and a number of online services, like legalzoom.com, will collect the information online and file the forms for you (for a fee, of course). If you want to do it all solo and are unsure about small details when filling out the form, the staff at the government office should, to an extent, be able to clarify certain points.

Finally, depending on your state, you may be required to file additional documents with your state tax board or franchise tax board. You generally have 30 to 90 days to file these subsequent forms, if they're required.

Insuring Your Company

Currently, it is wise to insure most aspects of life and all aspects of business. Liability litigation is serious and can financially cripple a growing company.

There is a plethora of different types of insurance available for all the different kinds of businesses and their respective company structures. Below you will find some insight into some of the types of insurance available for your business. Please note that this is not an exhaustive list, but further below will be instructions on how to find almost any type of coverage.

Property Insurance

This type of insurance is like home insurance; it covers your business' building and its contents against theft, fire, and, depending on your policy, natural disaster.

Vehicle Insurance

If your business will own and/or operate vehicles, vehicle insurance will help cover you for damages due to accidents or theft. It may cover injuries and offer protection against lawsuits filed against you by other drivers.

Public Liability Insurance

This covers you for harm or damages caused by your business to other people's property or person.

Professional Liability Insurance

This is popular with people offering consulting services such as lawyers, medical doctors, engineers, etc. This insurance covers damages sustained by a client by dint of your professional opinion/advice.

Business Continuation Insurance

If for reasons you can't foresee, your business slows down or shuts down, this type of insurance can compensate you while you get it back up and running.

Key Person Insurance

If you're a small business that has employees essential to its operation, and they stop working due to unforeseen circumstances, this insurance can help cover recruitment costs to replace them.

Shareholder Protection Insurance

Simply put, if a shareholder of your company passes away, this insurance will enable you to buy their now-available shares. This money can often be a good bereavement condolence for the family of the deceased and reduce possible complications from the stock holdings in the deceased's estate becoming a legal issue.

There are countless other types of insurance to consider, like employee liability insurance, workers' compensation insurance, business-specific types of insurance, etc. Knowing which policies your business should purchase is best decided by consulting your lawyer and/or an insurance broker. Insurance brokers will naturally want to sell you as many policies as they can, but they are very good at listing all the types of coverage your business may need.

How Do You Find Business Insurance?

- Research insurance providers; not all of them offer all the various policies.
- Once you find reputable companies set up meetings with brokers from serval firms (at least three different firms).
- Meet with the brokers to see what types of policies they can offer you and shop for the best rates.

Don't take insurance quotes at face value. Insurance policies will have different monthly premiums based on the cap on coverage, the deductible, and other factors. Ask your broker to break these down.

When shopping for insurance, you want to get a watertight (or airtight) policy. Oftentimes insurance companies will try their best to avoid paying a claim, because that's a loss on their balance sheets.

Here are some questions to ask the broker to help you craft a watertight policy:

- What exact type of damages does my policy cover?
- What scenarios would not be covered under my policy?

- Is there a way to be covered for any of these scenarios?
- How long does it generally take for a payout on my policy?
- In the event of a lawsuit, will the policy allow me to hire my own attorney, or must I use one recommended by the insurance firm?

It would be near impossible to exhaustively list the questions needed to be asked; multiple consultations with multiple brokers will aid you in understanding which issues are key and help you find and craft the most cost-efficient policy with the optimal coverage for your business' needs.

By now, you should have a better understanding of how to name, register, and protect your new business. Don't underestimate the importance of any of these steps as they can all be critical to the growth and success of your company. Maintain records and keep copies of all documents pertaining to your company registration and insurance policies. It is also wise to keep digital copies of key documents.

Chapter Eight: Hiring Team Members

Another important aspect of starting your own company is hiring your staff; this is a crucial part of building your company's front men. The first employees you hire are the most important ones; figuring out who they should be isn't exactly easy. But with the right mindset and plan, you'll be able to find the perfect candidates for the job.

Conducting Your First Skill Gap Analysis

Many new startups don't start off well if they skip this step; conducting your first one might be a little confusing if you haven't done it before, but it's essential to help your company get on its feet and moving forward.

The Overview of Your Company

Get a bird's eye view of every position and department that in your business by linking your business goals and company vision to a hierarchy chart. As the employer, use you can see what every position needs, skills-wise, to fill in the gaps with new employees.

Strategic Planning

You need to understand that you're going to go through a series of phases; the business world is always changing and evolving, so you must be ready for it. You need to be able to ascertain with certainty who you should hire and how you should train them to achieve your goals.

A thorough plan can help you with your analysis on two levels: on the individual level and on team level. If you had a workforce now, you'd get them together and talk about what the organization is missing. But since you're just starting up, you're going to jump ahead and find applicants that can fill in those gaps you have with the skills you're looking for. This will serve as groundwork and experience when the time comes to have that chat with your existing workforce.

Identifying Important Skills

Think of not only the skills necessary for the particular job slot, but skills your company would value and appreciate on an ongoing basis. This will help you immensely in narrowing down your applicants.

Measuring the Skills

You need to have a skills spreadsheet that is designed for every position. You don't need to be too strict with your criteria, since you're just starting up, but later you can be a little picky once you have a considerable presence in the business world.

Acting Upon Your Data

Now that you have talked with all the applicants and conducted your assessments, it's time to start hiring and training people. Your employees don't have to be the personification of perfection; you will all learn together along the way as your business is growing. Start choosing the ones you feel would be a good fit for your company, then train the ones that need a little push to be better.

Testing and Training:

Every job has a set of steps and ways to make it go smoothly, so you should test your possible employees on the specifics of the job to see how they would handle it. If they didn't show much aptitude on the test, but they've shown a lot of potential in a hands-on environment, then consider training them through training modules, practice sessions, and on-the-job training so they can get the experience they lack.

Finding People to Hire

This step can be difficult for most startups; thinking about the responsibility of being in charge of other people's livelihood can be scary. But if you manage to locate people that understand the level of risk involved in a startup, then you have nothing to worry about. Just be frank with every person you interview and share with them your idea and vision so they can get invested in it. Some avenues for finding those future employees:

Personal Referrals and Hiring Platforms

As a startup, you should be searching your personal network of people first, asking if anyone is interested or if they have a set of people that they might recommend. Posting on different platforms and social media can also bring in some applicants, just remember to specify what you want and go easy with your requirements.

Have an Online Presence

One of the things you should be doing is building your brand; this should be done early on because it's how you're going to get more people moving. People invest in something that has meaning and a good purpose, and you can show all that online to reach the maximum amount of people. You need exposure, so getting it on different platforms and social media is the way to go. People will be interested in this and want to be part of it; you just need to show them value and unique project ideas.

Don't Limit Yourself with Location Barriers

Even though it's easier to search locally, it's not always the right thing to do. You might need to break down geographical barriers and connect with people around the world. Some positions might be best filled by remote employees; some marketing angles or suppliers might call for an interpreter on the payroll.

The Educational System

Forming strong relationships with different colleges and universities can bring in top-tier candidates for you; think of it as having the professors or teachers to do the recruiting for you. Young graduates are motivated, hungry for knowledge, and smart with their bright new ideas. They would get a chance to be part of something interesting and could be one of the founding employees who are the cornerstone of your business.

The Interview Process

Remember to follow these specific ideals when you're interviewing people:

Assessing and Evaluating

Each person you interview needs to understand that this is the beginning of a journey; be honest with them about the possible risks, but also be open about the company's idea and your vision as an owner/employer. You need to see if they are eager to build this idea with you, show great potential and willingness to work on hard problems; you need people that like a challenge, that love the idea of being part of something new that could change the business world for the best.

Finding Potential

You will find it easier with time and practice to see the potential in people just from their first interview. Understanding their skills and passions and how a specific position can unleash their full potential can mean a lot for your business. You don't have to be focused on their track record, past successes, diplomas and degrees; you should see it in their eyes, in how they talk if they're truly interested and willing to go above and beyond for your company.

Key Traits to Consider

You should consider traits like multi-tasking, quick decision-making, being team players, being independent and strategic thinkers, and being a cultural fit. If you find people that embody these traits, then that can mean a lot to your business; you have strong, bold people who are not afraid, but if they are, then they won't keep it to themselves. You need people who have a voice and an ability to stand up and tell you something and how they feel the business would benefit from it. If they fully understand your vision and core values, any new idea that can further the process should be more than welcome.

You need to realize that finding these founding employees is extremely important, and you should ask them the right questions when you're conducting the interview. Here are some examples of what you should be asking your candidates:

Can You Describe Yourself?

This is important for you because it gives you a little more insight into the person you're talking to, understanding what makes them tick and what's important to them. You will know the person a little better based on their response to this question. This will help you when you narrow down your list of candidates, figuring out who was genuine and who is being cheesy or overdoing it.

In your opinion, what do you think your strengths and weaknesses are?

When you ask them about their strengths, you are getting an idea of their attributes that qualify them for the job. As for their weaknesses, that's a way to see if they can be honest and describe something in themselves that they know needs improvement.

Tell us about your last project - what went well and what didn't?

Leaving this question open-ended so they can choose what to talk about is great for seeing your potential employees using their own words to describe past successes or failures. You will get some insight into how they deal with hardships or sudden circumstances, listening to them talk about what they learned and what they should have done to avoid the problem.

What's the best advice you've received?

It's important to understand how well a person takes in input and criticism, that's why asking this question will let you know if they got some recently and how they handled it. Did they show understanding and take it under advisement? Or did they feel that they "are better than this", and show egocentric behavior?

Why do you believe you're a good fit for the company?

This question can give you an idea of why this candidate deserves the job by linking the answer to your company's goals and working environment. You will be able to gauge if there exists a mutual starting point for a good and beneficial professional relationship between both of you.

What can you do that can benefit us?

Their answer to this question, obviously, alerts you to specific ways they can contribute to your idea and cause.

What are your new ideas that you could apply to this position?

It's important to understand the job description and what one is supposed to do, but it's equally important to have the ability to think on one's feet. Creative ideas and thoughtful strategies can highly benefit a startup company like yours; their answer shows that they are willing to come up with solutions if the situation demands it.

What are you going to do if you don't get the job?

This might discourage your candidate, but it has a hidden motive; the question shows you who thought of alternatives and other steps that can help them reach their goal. This is a prime indicator as to how well they think out the future, possible risks, and contingency plans. This is a highly desirable mindset to have in your company.

Can you tell us something about...(anything unrelated)

You don't need to ask them this if you don't want to, but think about the stages in your company when it's just starting out. There might be times where people will do things that aren't exactly part of their job description, thinking out of the box and helping out just to keep things running smoothly. This is why the sudden change to an irrelevant question can give you an idea of how your applicants respond to changes that they didn't see coming. That's what makes a startup exciting, because the atmosphere will always be that way.

The Legalities

Now that you're going to hire people, it's time to do the paperwork and go through everything by the books that match your government's registration requirements, insurances, payroll, and tax forms. Here's a step-by-step list on how to do this right:

Employer Identification Number

You need to obtain this to use on the tax returns along with other documents to be submitted to the IRS or other tax administrations.

Proper Registration

You need to submit all the needed payments and documents to the labor department in your area; you must state unemployment compensation taxes. These taxes go to a relief fund that helps people who lose their jobs.

Workplace Safety Measures

You must have proper documentation that states you complied with the requirements of your locale's safety procedures and hazard-reduction terms as well as with the Occupational Safety and Health Act. You should keep safety records that have details regarding any workplace accidents or possible irregularities that can be submitted to your government's safety administrators.

Compensation Insurances

This might not be required of you since you're just a small company starting out, but that varies from one area to another. You need to have workers'-compensation coverage to protect your employees if they suffer on-the-job injuries. As a starting company, you can't afford any unnecessary lawsuits, so playing it safe is the way to go.

Employee Benefits

This purely depends on how much capital you have as an owner. Some startups might not have any benefits at first, like social events or health insurance, in which case it's still good to think about what you will need to do later in the way of benefits programs.

Report to the New Hire Reporting Agency

Each area or state has a reporting agency that helps the government track each new employee, do background checks, and see if they have past felonies or owe child support that they haven't paid yet.

Contracts

This is important because it will state everything that is required of you as an employer as well as what is required of the employees working for you. This contract would specify the job descriptions, probation periods, rules of the workplace, the net and gross salaries that they would be getting and how taxes will be processed by you as their employer.

Personal Records

It's important to have files such as tax forms, medical records, performance evaluations, and immigration status (if it applies) for every employee under your payroll.

Payroll

You need a proper system to withhold taxes, meaning that you withhold a portion of each employee's income for forwarding to the IRS or tax administrations. There should be forms like W-4 that each employee signs after filling out any allowances they're claiming for taxes; this helps you withhold the right amount from their monthly paychecks. Remember to prepare the W-2 forms that detail the annual filings to be submitted at the end of each year. Some companies have a banking system where the taxes go into their accounts on a monthly basis, or they have to go to the finance department and get the cash themselves. This depends on what kind of plan is perfect for you at the specific time; consider a software that can assist you in this to keep things from getting out of hand at some point.

Let's be frank, you are just starting up and entering an ocean full of big fish who think you're just a minnow. So, this isn't going to be easy for you at the beginning, but it's your job to attract the right people by showing them the true vision you have and the value you can provide. If you manage to get people that share your core values and understand your vision, then your business will boom with success.

Chapter Nine: Marketing & Promoting

Having people know who you are and what you stand for is key to your company's success; it will take time to get the exposure you need, but spreading the awareness about your brand is vital to getting more customers and clients to invest in your products and services. You need to think about your marketing strategy and how you can utilize the digital world to assist you, allowing you to reach more people faster.

Working on Your Brand

Branding is one of the major reasons why a company could succeed or fail; this is why you need to connect with your target audience and have them interested in your products and services. This will eventually lead to more purchases and subscriptions, so you need to differentiate your company with branding in the correct way.

The Target Market

One of the first steps to a successful branding process is figuring out who you're trying to reach. Ask yourself, who would be the audience with whom you'd want to share your vision? You need to understand that you can't succeed without your customers, so you must find the ideal ones that can be a part of your company's identity. There should be a relationship with your customers and clients wherein they can constantly give you feedback and opinions on how they perceived your products and services. You need people to have good experiences that they are quick to share with others, garnering you more customers in the process.

Investing in a Graphic Designer

This might be difficult for some startups, but it can be worth the investment. Try not to complicate things, though; it doesn't have to be super-perfect and flashy. Talk to your designer and explain your vision, story, and goals. He/she will be able to create multiple graphics that relate to all of it, allowing you to pick and choose those you think would be best. Friends or family that have a graphics-designing background might be much cheaper and easier for you but remember not to spare too many expenses because that can lead to difficulties in the future, possibly making you change everything and start from scratch again.

The Name and Image

Your next step is to come up with a decent visual language with a tagline that sticks, attracting people and making them turn heads to your logo, name, and slogan. You need something that looks appealing and makes a nice first impression. Try to be consistent, brief, and clear to every one of your targets; think about creating something resonates within the people, something that isn't too bold, macho, corny, vague, or forgettable. Also, people don't connect with generic names that much these days, so you should think about creating something with a made-up word that can possibly be the language of your company, one that matches a catchy slogan and keeps it memorable.

Create Great Experiences

This might be hard at first because your company is still a newcomer in the business world, but later this will be one of the reasons why people like you and want to continue investing in you. You should make something for them that they would remember, something that can make you stand out from your competitors. You might consider being a cause-driven company that people relate to because you are showing that you care. Or you could do something that defies expectations, doing something that might be unorthodox and fresh. But be careful not to make people upset, that might backfire right back at you, especially when you're starting out.

Getting Involved in the Local Community

This might not be possible for you at the beginning, but if you do this right, you could be looking at a whole new level of awareness. People won't forget about you if you do something that benefits the community they live in; it helps raise your business profile among all your potential customers. To be involved, you could start donating to a local charity group or doing volunteer work to help them out. Or you could sponsor local events, giving the impression that your company is community oriented. You could contribute to a fundraiser for a local hospital or school; there are any number of ways to make the locals like you more and feel comfortable with your brand because they can trust you and your morals.

Your Business Website

It is a pivotal step to create a website for your company, and if you don't have one, then you'd be missing out on a lot of opportunities and possible leads. Let's take a look at why it's so important to have one:

- Credibility and showing people that you are a legit company.

- It helps your business grow by accomplishing various marketing strategies.

- It generates more feedback from customers to be better.

- Gives your clients and possible new leads a chance to contact you or purchase something you offer.

- Brings in healthy traffic through different SEO (Search Engine Optimization) tactics that can increase your exposure and possible deals.

- It increases your presence and visibility online and in general.

- It helps you save money on big marketing campaigns because it's cost-effective.

- Customers have 24/7 access to what they want, whether it's information, support, and news on upcoming products.
- You will see a considerable boost in sales through your online shop features.
- It increases your overall reputation.
- It gives you a chance to make royalty programs and reward schemes.
- You can add testimonials and facts from different clients later along the road to increase opportunities for leads and profits, showing everyone how good you are.
- It helps you level the playing field against bigger multinational corporations when it comes to rankings.
- Ease of access and convenience that makes people's lives much easier, which will more likely lead to more sales and profits.
- You can show people your vision, telling your story easily to people overseas.
- It would be a way for people to subscribe to weekly newsletters or notifications about new products and discounts.

Marketing Your Business

Let's be honest, you need inexpensive ways to get maximum awareness and cover a huge scale of the market with your presence. This is why digital marketing can be your number-one method of reaching people.

You're your own boss now, and an entrepreneur that wants to see results from your hard work; getting those results would be much easier if you utilized the digital world. Here are some ways of utilizing the digital world to get those results:

Social Media

This is one of the strongest and most effective ways to market a business these days; almost every one of your customers and potential new ones have an account on one, two, or several social media channels. Whether it's Twitter, Facebook, and/or Instagram, a social-media portal is considered to be the easiest method to enhance your online presence and help you generate a big percentage of leads. It can be done through a series of posts that are both creative and appealing, so people don't scroll down and ignore it. Create fun and engaging questions, submit videos related to your business and idea, keep things interesting by posting every day to keep people reeled into your page. You can engage with your audience easily and build strong connections; this leads to more loyal customers that follow you and what you post. You should show everyone that you care by answering everyone's questions and concerns; you can establish brand awareness, and more people will know what type of services and products you're offering. You can expand your business in various ways thanks to social media, so use it to market your brand and get more prospects.

Mobile

74% of people in the world use their smartphones to search for something they need. Therefore, you should have your website mobile-friendly; that can radically increase the number of visitors that check your website. Optimizing your platforms and strategies to be compatible with mobile can mean a lot for your business. You can have small ads on popular apps that people use every day; people are bound to see your name and brand as they're using their phones.

Another way of marketing yourself through the mobile world would be something to consider in the future, when your business has solidified its position and you have the funds for it: you could create your own mobile app, something that relates to your business or service that you're offering.

Email

This is a strong method of promoting your business by tailoring emails specifically to each customer; you can do this by knowing what the customer wants and needs, then allowing them to get it. People love personalized emails that are directly based on what they're after at a specific time; if they're searching for something similar to what you have to offer and you hand it to them on a silver platter, the sale is a done deal. Eventually, these people will become your frequent and loyal customers, investing in your services and purchasing your products.

Marketing automation methods are still an important part of promoting your business easily and you won't have to pay outrageous amounts to reach people. You can nurture your customers with follow-ups and new things that would interest them by syncing everyone's profile with your current CRM system. That way, they would be placed into your workflow, and the correct emails would be sent to the right people.

Special Offers

People love good deals; it might mean less money for each product you sell, but the sales volume going through the roof would surely ease the pain. You increase your profits over time that way.

The methods you could apply range from discounts, seasonal offers, and special coupons sent through emails or mobile ads, to offers for people to buy in bulk to get it all at a lower per-item price.

The discounts could be small codes given to them as they purchase something or sent to them through their emails to use later. Your coupons can be physical ones or E-coupons if you want it to be more convenient for them, saving you a little money in the process, too. A seasonal or special occasion is the perfect time for you to implement some discount offers. That's why there are so many great deals offered at Christmas time; the pros know that a huge boost in sales volume easily outweighs a small decrease in sales margins.

The Approach to Your Customers

If you're thinking about what kind of business you're planning to be, have you thought about being a customer-driven company? People love it when they feel they have been heard and supported every time they have a concern, request, or specific feedback. As an entrepreneur that wants to change the world of business, you can start by showing people that you offer more than just some goods or services; you offer the value that people can appreciate and a brand that they can trust. It's just the way of things in the business world; happy customers mean more referrals, increased sales, extra exposure, immense growth, and plenty of profits. This is exactly what your business would need to move forward and boom with success.

Handling Reviews

This is extremely important because you want people to be heard, thanked, and supported, especially when it's a bad review. Do not shun or ignore unpleasant reviews because that would be a sign of not caring about what people think; you are bound to upset some people along the way because, sadly, we cannot appease every single person in the world all the time. So, the way to handle an unpleasant review is to thank them for their feedback, apologizing for any inconvenience or for their bad experience.

Then you should contact these people who wrote the bad reviews and get a better understanding of what happened and how they feel about it; remember to be calm, supportive, and never accuse people or get defensive. Try as hard as you can to either solve the problem or compensate them in any way possible; this will increase your image by showing people that you care. As for the good reviews, you should reply in kind and thank them for their kind words and loyalty. I know this is difficult but try to not sound too robotic with your replies.

Customer Service and Complaints

Do you know why most startups fail so soon? One of the reasons is not having a proper customer service plan that caters to people that need assistance or need to file a complaint. Let's dive into how you should respond to people with complaints or concerns through the famous five P's in customer care:

Professional

You must focus on rectifying the issue or problem, not the customer's tone or behavior; you should be sincere and humble in your responsive. So, you should never lash out or become hostile with the customer. Ask them for more details and listen to every word, then reiterate it in your own words to make sure that this is what they said and to prove that you listened. Remember to always try to see the problem from the customer's point of view.

Prompt

You shouldn't let a negative comment hang in the air for long without being answered; your window of reply should be within 24-to-48 hours, maximum. People need to feel that their problem is acknowledged, even if you don't have a solution to it, just reply to let them know that they've been heard.

Personal

People hate it when they get a robotic or automated response; they want to hear something genuine, friendly, and respectful. People like it when they are heard, validated, and made to feel justified. Try to be normal and approachable and use simple words that are easy to follow and understand, make them feel at ease and believe that you care about resolving this issue for them.

Polite

It's difficult for some people to stay calm and professional when they get negative comments; you might take it personally and get angry but remember that it's not your place to judge. Even if the customer is being unreasonable or unfair with their comments, you should never reply thoughtlessly with haste and anger. Remember to see the issue from their perspective; you should show empathy and compassion because that's how they would calm down. Remember to apologize, even if it's not your fault.

Private

Remember that people want to be validated and heard, but it doesn't always require a public conversation for everyone to see. Respond and acknowledge them for sure but invite them to have a little chat privately either by phone or email. There are some cases where discretion is needed, and you must judge the situation, whether it requires a private or public response. Also, people feel comfortable and talk freely when it's private and not visible to thousands of people watching.

It would be awful if you created an amazing and useful idea, but you can't make anyone notice what you've created, or it's not appealing at all for people to try what you have to offer. That's why promoting and branding is crucial; every startup can face a lot of problems when it comes to marketing and without it, the business might fail drastically, so remember to put in a lot of thought on how you're going to let people see you and remember you. Also, focus on customer care and make them feel heard.

Chapter Ten: Scaling & Growing

Starting the business is the easy part — ok, it's not exactly easy, but things tend to get more complicated as we move forward. Getting past initial challenges in terms of finances, paperwork, and documentation, and hiring the right team is one thing, but growing the business is a whole other ballgame.

It doesn't matter if it's a bakery, law firm, or online store. As a business owner, you want to grow and expand — and in turn, reach more people and make more money. This is the end goal for any business owner, or at least the serious ones. It's not about having an extra income for the sake of it; that business is your baby, and just like an actual one, there comes a time where it needs to grow and flourish.

A lot of business owners try to bite off more than can chew, and they end up hindering the progress of the company instead of taking it forward. Like anything else in life, timing is everything. Whether it's asking the girl you like out or scaling up your business, you need to find just the right moment, and that can be a bit tricky. Fortunately, there are some signs and indicators that it is time — and now might be the moment when you can start working on growing and expanding the business to take it to the next level.

Signs That it Might be A Time to Scale Your Business

Demand and supply

One of the biggest mistakes some small businesses do is trying to expand without making sure they have it figured out in terms of demand and supply. You might be achieving some impressive numbers right now, but that doesn't mean that will continue to happen in the future. This is why you need to thoroughly consider whether or not you have enough demand – and supply – to support your efforts to grow.

Scaling your business is expensive, and it will cost you a lot of money and effort. The question is, can your current and, more importantly, future projected supply help you get there? If the answer is yes, then this is the first sign that you might be ready to scale your business. But you really need to be certain of the answer to this question, because it quite literally might save you from going bankrupt while trying to expand. Do you have enough customers right now? Do you expect to get more in the future at a consistent rate than ensures you'll have steady cash flow while trying to grow your business? These aren't the kind of questions you could answer overnight. You need to do thorough research and accurate forecasts to predict whether you can not only maintain your current level but also exceed it while trying to expand.

On the other hand, it's not just the demand that you should take into consideration. You might be getting all the demand you need, and then some, but you can't supply. Can your business/small factory/store cover your current and future needs? It would be nonsensical to try and open a new store or in a different city or country when you can barely cover the current requests you get on a regular basis. This brings us to the following point.

Having enough manpower

Scaling your business requires being able to support your efforts with the necessary experienced manpower. Sure, you can hire new people wherever it is you're trying to expand, but they can't exactly get going on their own — they'll need training, and people who know the business processes to teach and guide them. Think of it that way, if you only have two people running your entire operations — each with a very specific and important role that is indispensable — does it really make sense to send one over to the new location and hope the other can handle all business operations on their own? It definitely wouldn't. But if you have enough team members to carry on with the job even if some of their colleagues got preoccupied with something else, then yeah, it might be a good idea to go for some scaling up.

Finances are good

Needless to say, trying to grow your business with insufficient funds is a bad idea that will not end well for you or the business. You must make sure your finances are in order before you try scaling up because, as we mentioned earlier, expansion is costly, and it will require some significant investment on your side. We talked about the importance of projected demand, but you need to consider other factors in the equation if we're talking about expansion.

Even if you can and will get the required supply in the future that can sustain you, will the money coming off those deals be enough? Are you trying to go overseas, and there's a currency change which might even cost you more? What will happen if there is an unforeseen obstacle, and how will you deal with it? In other words, you can't just rely on the fact that you will have enough demand in the future. You need to do the math and make sure that demand can sustain you financially while taking into consideration other factors like currency fluctuations and conversions, emergencies, and unexpected costs. This is why it is advisable that you only go forward if you are 100% certain your finances are good and can, in fact, sustain your growth plan. It helps if you already have an emergency fund that you can tap into in case things go south.

Original goals are exceeded

Any business starting out sets certain goals. They can be anything from reaching certain numbers to covering initial investments. Another indicator that it may be time to scale is reaching and exceeding those previous goals. But they need to be the big ones you set for yourself when you first started out — paying your employees' salaries on time isn't exactly an indicator you should try scaling. If you find that your business is consistently reaching and exceeding any goals it sets for itself, then perhaps scaling is the solution.

You cannot let your company linger in a comfort zone, because it can be extremely difficult to get out of those. You need the challenge because this is how you, the employees, and the company grow and learn. So, once you're there, and goals are met, start setting higher ones pertaining to an expansion plan that will help you scale up and reach new heights, achieving those new targets and then moving on to even greater ones.

Your team is ready

The most valuable asset a company has is its people, and you can't possibly move forward with your plans to expand and grow without making sure your people are ready for such a step. This doesn't just pertain to their performance and numbers, but what they think and need. It's imperative that you conduct meetings with your people, from middle and upper management to regular employees. Ask them what their problems are and what they think about current plans to grow. You need their input, and you can rest assured they will have useful input — after all, it's they who do the job. Their insight can help you alter your plans, if necessary, and come up with new strategies.

People might be resistant to change, and if your team is not on board, then maybe you should rethink your decision to scale up right now. You could hire some fresh blood who would be more susceptible to change and infuse them with old members to help smoothen the transition. The important thing is having the majority of your team on board, because you are going to need them.

One more angle that you need to cover when it comes to your team is making sure your people are up to date with technology. We live in a world driven by technology, and any business relies heavily on it, one way or another. And before you can scale up, you have to make sure that your company is using the proper and most recent technology.

Factors Hindering Attempts to Scale Up and Grow

Being behind on technology

Picking up from our last point, if your company is using obsolete technology, you probably stand no chance of expansion and growth. You can rest assured that your competition is using the latest technologies and solutions, and if you want to keep up and conquer new markets, you must do the same. It can be anything from cloud solutions to AI and internet marketing strategies; just find out what technologies you need to grow your business and start training your people to leverage them before you even consider scaling up. We live in a digital age, and a company that wants to expand needs to be leveraging state-of-the-art technologies to make it happen.

Rushing the process

We talked about the importance of doing studies and crunching the numbers to figure out just how well you'll do in the future in terms of demand, supply, and finances. A lot of businesses, unfortunately, try to skip past those steps and rush into the process of scaling the company and expanding without proper studies and calculations. The problem is, rushing things without careful consideration not only promises poor results for the scaling up, but it also jeopardizes the integrity of what you've built so far.

It happens quite often that companies rush into expanding to new markets and find halfway through the process that they don't have enough funding to do it. So, they start tapping into reserves and company funds, leading to catastrophic results like not being to pay your bills or even the salaries. As a result of poor planning and rash decision making, the company might have to declare bankruptcy. So, impulsively trying to scale up the company can lead to failure on all fronts.

Not doing market research

The bottom line is, you're presenting a service or a product to consumers. And if you don't know what those consumers want, the entire process is doomed to failure. While you may have done proper market research before starting your business, you need to do it again before trying to expand. If you're trying to conquer a new market, you must ask yourself, is there even room for what I'm offering? Do the people there really need my services? If you want to add a new line of products, for example, you can't do so on a whim. You must be 100% certain there is demand for that product, and that people will buy it.

This is why it's important to conduct thorough market research before any steps to expand your business. The last thing you need is trying to invade a saturated market or offering a new product/service that no one really needs or even asked for. Running a business should never be subject to personal opinions and prejudices, but rather thorough research and careful planning.

Poor infrastructure

One of the biggest reasons why businesses fail in their expansion attempts is not having the proper infrastructure and processes in place before embarking on such a step. Any company starting out needs quite some time to figure things out and come up with its own process, from how people log in their time out/in to how they receive and perform their daily assignments. If those processes, both simple and intricate, are not properly in place, your expansion has no hope of success.

From continuous training to productivity tracking and quality assurance, everything needs to be in place, and all the boxes must be ticked before you try to open a new branch or merge with another company. Chaos is the one thing that can plunge the company into failure, and order does the exact opposite.

How to Scale Your Business
Evaluating your options

The first step to trying to scale your business is evaluating your options and carefully planning what the next step is going to be. We talked about the importance of figuring out your finances and employee readiness, but there are several other factors that you need to consider. For starters, how do you want to scale up your business? Expansion needs thorough preparations and planning, but you first need to figure out which in direction you'd like to take your business. Are you looking to increase your sales by introducing a new product or enforcing a new strategy? Do you want to open a new branch somewhere else? Or are you looking to merge your company with another?

It's important that you evaluate your options to find which direction is best for your business in the long run. Then, as mentioned earlier, you should move to evaluate the readiness of your people, your finances, and future projections. Again, the success of your scaling up attempts rests solely on how well you plan for it and evaluate your different options. So, take it slowly and cover all the angles, because the slightest misstep puts your entire company in jeopardy.

Getting the funding

Earlier in this chapter, we talked about the importance of having it figured in terms of supply and demand, as well as having your finances in order. But what if all the other signs are there and everything is good to go, except for funding? In that case, if funding is really the one thing stopping your business from growing and expanding, then you should consider getting it from alternative sources.

Fortunately, we live in a time where entrepreneurship is on the rise, and there are a lot of willing parties that can help your company grow and reach its potential. Take angel investors and accelerators, for instance, who usually supply smaller companies with the necessary funds for such expansion in exchange for equity. You also have small business contests where they compete for a cash prize that could be anything from $10,000 to $100,000, like the FedEx

Small Business Grant Contest. Entering those contests, you don't need to give equity to anyone; just present a kickass plan and impress the judges, and the prize would be yours.

You could also go for a loan, though that should be your last resort. But they sometimes really help and can procure you the funding you need to expand and grow your business. The important thing is not letting funding get in the way of your company's growth and expansion if everything else says it's the right time to start.

Network

No matter what approach you plan on taking with your business expansion, networking is a crucial angle in which you'll need to excel. Scaling a company up is about connections and the people you know, and the more you grow your networks and meet new people who could help you, the better your chances will be. True, you need to be good at what you're doing, but expanding a company requires knowing the right people to help you achieve your goals. Go to social events, startup competitions, and summits, and reach out to mentors and experienced individuals. This will help you form a powerful network that will put you in another city — or even country — or inspire you to come up with new ideas to grow your business.

Hiring the right staff

You have two major assets in your quest for expansion: the people and the technology. If one of those two pillars is missing, your chances of scaling your business up are slim to none. We've already talked about technology and how you need to use the latest in order to stay in the game, but without people to use that technology, it will be worthless. You need to rely on your current team, yes, but you will probably need to hire some new people to help you achieve your goals. If you can't find the exact quality you need right now, maybe it is time to consider outsourcing some of your departments. For instance, expansion requires having a dedicated and professional customer service team, which you might have not had in your current structure. It would definitely take a lot of time to interview, hire, and train customer service personnel, so in a case like this, it'd be best to outsource the entire process.

That way, you'll get pre-trained agents who know how to handle customers, and all you would need to do is train them in *your* process and how to handle the specific details of *your* company. You'll most likely be saving money as well because outsourced services tend to be a lot cheaper.

Dream big

While this might be something taken out of one of those self-development books, in truth, dreaming big is one of the most crucial angles to scaling up your business. If your company is currently worth one million dollars, what's to stop it from being worth ten or a hundred million? If you are going to expand, set high goals for yourself, because if you aim big and put in the effort and time, you'll make it. This won't happen overnight, and it will take a lot of blood, sweat, and tears, but with the right mindset and experienced team, you can get there.

Growing your business might be the most challenging aspect of your entire journey, but it is worth it. To see your team grow in front of you and more people getting to know your brand are things that will make all the time and effort you spent on this process worthwhile. The important thing is giving this phase its due planning and putting in the time and effort to ensure it will work out without undue complications.

Conclusion

In the last decade, an entrepreneurial revolution has been on the rise. Although there are more than 400,000 entrepreneurs to date, only fifty percent of new companies survive the rising competition. Possibly, one of the many reasons why entrepreneurship has become so popular is because today's post-industrial business world is almost completely reliant on the internet. And that doesn't just apply to networking. There are now classes dedicated entirely to the study of entrepreneurship, paving the way for new independent business owners to introduce their products and services to the market.

Perhaps our era's consistent economic decline was what inspired this sudden rise of business startups in the last few decades. More individuals are now coming to realize just how much more lucrative it is to leave their nine-to-five jobs behind and work on their own startup, while the appeal of becoming one's own boss undoubtedly remains a factor in this so-called "startup revolution".

This phenomenon may leave many wondering whether this is just another ephemeral fad in the business world that will inevitably die mainly because of the number of failing startups in the market, some of which don't survive more than a few months. But the underlying cause of these failures is certainly not a flaw in the revolution itself but is due to the media's elusive portrayal of how business moguls have come to succeed. Many an aspiring business owner has attempted to start a business from scratch based purely on the kind of business myths that threaten every entrepreneur.

These myths usually revolve around a warped idea of following one's passion, selling ideas to the first investor you come across, and creating a business with limited knowledge of market demands and basic business development know-how. That said, many entrepreneurs start businesses as an escape from corporate life. And while a successful business doesn't have to be completely unique, solely staring a business to jump on a trending bandwagon is one of the reasons behind many business failures.

This book has covered the importance of other aspects than good business ideas, but that's only because they tend to be overlooked. That surely doesn't mean that an individual with no coherent business model and goal, other than a quick way to make money, will see success. On the other hand, entrepreneurial success is not as challenging as many of today's publications may make it seem.

You'll often see some staggering numbers of failing businesses that never got to see the light despite their promising goals and ideas, but that's usually because the founders of such businesses lacked the skills needed for their business. Most business ideas are born out of need – future founders run into a problem with no immediate solution and decide to create one, for themselves as well as the public. The initial enthusiasm that sparks out of that ah-ha moment usually instills a sense of impatience and irrational anxiety. Oftentimes, entrepreneurs want to implement their ideas as quickly as they can before anyone else makes the same discovery, though the chances of that are slim. And the hasty decisions that arise from this impatience is what eats through the potential of what could have been a billion-dollar idea.

On the other hand, many aspiring entrepreneurs are aware of the importance of developing a compelling business model and dedicate years to the process of perfecting a solution to a problem before they begin their search for possible funding sources. While going into the nitty-gritty of a product before launching it is certainly a smart move, future founders should always cash in as soon as they build a basic business model. This is primarily because cashflow issues may take years to be resolved but should ideally be dealt with simultaneously with product development to shorten the time it takes for the company to launch.

Of course, business prototypes should always be offered to the public on a small scale for feedback before launching, which is another reason why a startup may fail. On the other hand, founders don't have to wait until their service or product is completely impeccable before they make it accessible. Many startups offer reasonably ready services and immediately amend anything that customers complain about.

All these issues that entrepreneurs run into may be the cause of failure, but it's certainly not because entrepreneurship is going out of fashion, or because recent graduates have abused the entrepreneurship path. In fact, all these new companies that offer outstanding solutions to the public are increasingly changing the industry for the better. There is no limit to just how many successful startups penetrate the market, but only those who develop the skills needed for their business thrive. This is possibly the only obstacle that may be standing in your way.

While this book has been written essentially to help new entrepreneurs succeed, the best way to avoid failure is by familiarizing yourself with *why* startups fail. It's certainly not because some founders are luckier than others, and it's not a matter of being discovered and running into just the right people that would help you on your road to success. The only individuals you should count on are your partners and yourself. Business success is an equation that can be learned, and that's what this book aims to help teach you.

Reading as many sources as you can on the field of your choice will be your handy tools before you begin developing your idea. If you already have an idea in mind, build a basic prototype and ask for critique from your trusted partners before you begin your search for potential investors.

Finally, always bear in mind that in some rare cases, the current market will not yet be ready for your product. Many founders who have been ahead of their time with their innovative solutions have eventually found success when they chose to launch at just the right time. Sometimes, products are best kept in development until the market need for them arises.

www.ingramcontent.com/pod-product-compliance
Lightning Source LLC
Chambersburg PA
CBHW062111220526
45471CB00010B/3691